THE GAME'S AFOOT

SHERLOCK HOLMES PLAYS

OTHER BOOKS BY MICHAEL & MOLLIE HARDWICK INCLUDE:

The Sherlock Holmes Companion
The Charles Dickens Companion
The Man Who Was Sherlock Holmes
Four Sherlock Holmes Plays
Sherlock Holmes Investigates
(all published by John Murray)
Writers' Houses: A Literary Journey in England
(Phoenix House)
Alfred Deller: A Singularity of Voice
(Cassell)

The Game's Afoot

SHERLOCK HOLMES PLAYS BY

MICHAEL & MOLLIE HARDWICK

FROM STORIES BY

SIR ARTHUR CONAN DOYLE

JOHN MURRAY
Fifty Albemarle Street London

Printed in Great Britain by
Cox & Wyman Ltd,
London, Reading and Fakenham

Cased 7195 1925 X
Limp 7195 1924 1

FOREWORD

This volume owes its existence to the success of its predecessor, *Four Sherlock Holmes Plays*, published in 1964. To our pleasure, and our publisher's, that collection rapidly achieved a five-figure circulation and continues to sell steadily, chiefly to schools where the plays are studied in class and performed at end-of-term. We have heard of productions as far away as New Zealand and the United States, and a television company in Holland made screen versions, which, considering that we adapted the stage texts largely from our radio dramatisations of the original stories, was surely a long way round to travel.

The five years since *Four Sherlock Holmes Plays* appeared have coincided with a wave of Sherlockian activity, especially in Great Britain. We have had two long series on BBC Television and several on radio, the publication of several fresh studies of the stories and of Sir Arthur Conan Doyle, and, most vivid of all in the memory of those of us fortunate enough to have taken part, the great costume tour of Switzerland in the footsteps of Sherlock Holmes, which gained world-wide notice. The letters we have had from young viewers and listeners following the televising or broadcasting of our scripts have confirmed afresh, both in enthusiasm and criticism, that Holmes and Watson are fully as popular with younger generations as with older, are thought as worthy as ever of serious study, and are regarded as being far from 'old hat' in the Space Age. It is especially gratifying that there are more young faces than ever to be seen at any gathering of the Sherlock Holmes Society of London.

We hope the appearance of this new volume will prove timely, both to those who have used its predecessor and those who have not. At any rate, it has again been a great pleasure to prepare.

MICHAEL & MOLLIE HARDWICK

CONTENTS

The authors wish to express their gratitude to the Trustees of the Estate of the late Sir Arthur Conan Doyle

NOTES FOR PRODUCERS

As in *Four Sherlock Holmes Plays*, the texts of these acting versions have been kept as free as possible from precise directions for staging and acting. Much of their use, we know, lies in classroom reading; but they can be staged both in the classroom, with the most makeshift settings of desks and chairs, and in the theatre, as elaborately as the producer's resources and ingenuity will allow.

In writing a play for television, the most careful regard must be paid to the mechanics of every bit of 'business', leaving nothing vague, nothing to chance in a highly technical operation involving dozens of people and thousands of pounds. This, for example, is a brief passage from the 'camera script' of our BBC-TV dramatisation of *The Sign of Four*:

86. 3 E

CMS on object Alcove-wall BUDDHA behind MARY	I trust you have no objection to tobacco smoke – the balsamic odour of Eastern tobacco?
Slow ZOOM OUT TO MS MARY	MARY: None at all. Please, Mr. Sholto . . .

87. 5

REVERSE M2S MARY THAD fav. him	
CRAB & LOOSEN, PAN R. collect WATSON & HOLMES bring object on	THADDEUS: Too gracious. I am a little nervous and I find it an invaluable sedative.
fg table into L.fg END IN LS GROUP	(WATSON GIVES HOLMES A SIGNIFICANT GLANCE)

All that, just to put across a few lines. In contrast, the producers of these four plays may be as free as they like to elaborate upon what we have set down as the simplest and most economical way of presenting them before an audience. We see a play's producer as a catalyst – an intermediary, knowledgeable adviser, objective viewer and technical expert – upon the author's text, which is the essence of the play, and the actors' interpretation of their roles. Professional actors and actresses bring to rehearsals wide experience and developed instinct: the producer of amateurs with little or no experience is in the much more creative position of having to mould from the rawest material, and we hope we are helping him by not laying down the equivalent of those tapes and chalk marks which govern every inch of movement of actors on television, but leaving him free to use these texts as the basis for what he can contrive.

May we repeat our plea from the preceding volume that these plays should be acted 'straight' – that is, without any element of burlesque or melodrama? In the same way that the comedies of Gilbert and Sullivan remain sparkling and funny in their own right, but become ludicrous when attempts are made to improve on them or 'send them up', so Sherlock Holmes and Dr. Watson should be left to their immortal qualities. We confess to having made many small changes from the original dialogue, time-sequences, and so forth: these are essential in translating the printed word into the spoken and making it possible to act what was meant only to be read. In the case of a few changes we can claim no technical necessity, but must plead, for better or worse, our personal dramatic instinct. The adapter's chief responsibility is to retain at all costs the spirit of the original, even if the letter has to be expressed in somewhat new terms; and this we see as the producer's and actors' duty, too.

Good luck with these plays – and if you are staging one and would care to invite us, we should like to come, time and geography permitting. Every production we have seen so far has been quite different from the others and we have learned something from them all.

THE THREE GARRIDEBS

SCENE I: 221B Baker Street, *evening*
SCENE II: Nathan Garrideb's study, *that evening*
SCENE III: Messrs. Holloway and Steele's Estate Agency, *next morning*
SCENE IV: Scotland Yard, *that morning*
SCENE V: Nathan Garrideb's study, *that afternoon*

Characters in order of appearance:

DR. WATSON

SHERLOCK HOLMES

MRS. HUDSON: Their housekeeper. Middle-aged and perhaps Scottish. She dotes on them, but despairs of Holmes's habits.

JOHN GARRIDEB: 'A short, powerful man with the round, fresh, clean-shaven face characteristic of so many American men of affairs. The general effect was chubby and rather childlike, so that one received the impression of quite a young man with a broad set smile upon his face... His accent was American, but was not accompanied by any eccentricity of speech.'

MRS. SAUNDERS: Nathan Garrideb's housekeeper. Perhaps young and rather blowsy, to contrast her with Mrs. Hudson.

NATHAN GARRIDEB: 'A very tall, loose-jointed, round-backed person, gaunt and bald, some sixty-odd years of age...

Large round spectacles and a small projecting goat's beard combined with his stooping attitude to give him an expression of peering curiosity. The general effect, however, was amiable, though eccentric.'

MR. HOLLOWAY'S CLERK: A very deferential young man.

MR. HOLLOWAY: Rather oily.

A UNIFORMED CONSTABLE: Portly and majestic.

INSPECTOR LESTRADE: 'A quick and energetic worker, despite his adherence to conventional methods to the exclusion of inspiration.' Sallow, rat-faced, dark-eyed . . . In his forties. An unrefined accent.

THE THREE GARRIDEBS

[*N.B. In this play the same set will serve for all five scenes, without need of black-out or lowering the curtain. The few necessary adjustments, it will be found, are made by characters in the action, so the basic properties may be confined to little more than a table, three chairs and a picture-hook in the back wall. On the floor will need to be a small mat concealing a board, which in the last scene, will represent a trapdoor*]

SCENE ONE

[*The parlour of* 221B *Baker Street. The lamp is lit on the table, on which is a tray bearing glasses and a decanter.* WATSON *is seated, contentedly puffing his pipe and reading a newspaper, occasionally refreshing himself from a glass. A telephone directory lies to hand. The picture-hook is occupied by a portrait of Queen Victoria.* HOLMES, *wearing his old dressing-gown over his clothes, enters, pipe in mouth and reading a letter which he has just taken from its envelope*]

WATSON: Ah, Holmes!

HOLMES: My dear Watson, here's a chance for you to make some money.

WATSON: Eh? Well, don't keep me waiting. What is it?

[HOLMES *sits opposite* WATSON, *who fills a glass and passes it over*]

HOLMES: Have you ever heard the name Garrideb?

WATSON: Garrideb?

HOLMES: G-A-R-R-I-D-E-B.

WATSON: There is no such name.

HOLMES [*waving the letter at* WATSON]: Let's hope there is, for your sake. If you can lay hands on a Garrideb, there is money in it.

[WATSON *quickly picks up the telephone directory and turns pages*]

WATSON: Soon see what the telephone directory has to offer. What's it all about, Holmes?

HOLMES: It's a long story – rather a whimsical one, too. I don't think that in all our adventures together we have ever come across anything more singular.

WATSON: Here you are! [*Reads*] 'Garrideb, N. 136 Little Ryder Street.'

HOLMES: Is he the only one?

WATSON: Er, yes.

HOLMES: Then I'm sorry to disappoint you. That is the man who has written me this letter. We want another to match him.

[*Knock on door*]

WATSON: Confound it, Holmes, I wish . . . Come in!

[MRS. HUDSON *enters, carrying a card tray*]

Yes, Mrs. Hudson?

MRS. HUDSON: A visitor, Mr. Holmes.

HOLMES [*taking the card and glancing at it*]: Mr. John Garrideb.

WATSON: *John* Garrideb!

HOLMES: Ask him to step up, Mrs. Hudson.

MRS. HUDSON [*going*]: Yes, sir.

[HOLMES *passes* WATSON *the card*]

WATSON [*reads*]: 'John Garrideb, Counsellor at Law, Moorville, Kansas, United States of America!'

HOLMES [*chuckling*]: A second Garrideb, Watson. But this gentleman is in the plot already, I'm afraid.

WATSON: Plot?

HOLMES: I certainly didn't expect to see him this evening, but he'll be able to tell us a good deal that I need to know.

MRS. HUDSON [*returning*]: Mr. Garrideb, sir.

HOLMES: Come in, sir. Come in!

[MRS. HUDSON *exits as* JOHN GARRIDEB *enters*]

JOHN GARRIDEB: Mr. Sherlock Holmes? Ah, yes! Your pictures aren't unlike you, if you don't mind my saying so.

[*They shake hands*]

HOLMES: Not at all. This is my friend and colleague, Dr. Watson.

WATSON: How d'ye do?

[*They shake hands,* WATSON *gestures to the vacant chair.* GARRIDEB *sits*]

JOHN GARRIDEB: Pleased to know you, gentlemen. Now, Mr. Holmes, I believe you've had a letter from my namesake, Mr. Nathan Garrideb?

HOLMES: I have had such a letter. [*Holding it up*] I take it you are the Mr. John Garrideb referred to in it?

JOHN GARRIDEB: Sure I am.

HOLMES: I see you have been in England for some time.

JOHN GARRIDEB [*suspiciously*]: What makes you say that?

HOLMES: Your clothes. Your whole outfit is English.

JOHN GARRIDEB [*laughs*]: Well, I've read of your tricks, Mr. Holmes, but I never guessed I'd be the subject of them. Now, how do you figure that out?

HOLMES: Quite simply. The shoulder cut of your coat, the toes of your boots – could anyone doubt it?

JOHN GARRIDEB: Well, well, well! Yes, business brought me over here some little time ago. But say, I guess we didn't meet to talk about the cut of my socks. [*Hardening*] What about getting down to that paper there in your hand?

HOLMES: Patience! Patience, Mr. Garrideb! Dr. Watson would tell you that these little digressions of mine sometimes have some bearing on the matter.

WATSON: Quite true.

HOLMES: Tell me, why did the other Mr. Garrideb – Mr. Nathan Garrideb – not come with you?

JOHN GARRIDEB [*flaring*]: That guy! Why did he ever drag you into it at all? Here was a bit of professional business between two gentlemen, and one of them goes and writes to a detective! I saw him this morning. He told me this fool-trick he'd played, and that's why I'm here now.

HOLMES: I fancy it was simply zeal on his part to help you both achieve your object. And I understand that's equally vital for you both.

JOHN GARRIDEB: Huh!

HOLMES: He knew I had means of getting information. So it was very natural that he should apply to me.

JOHN GARRIDEB [*mollified*]: Well, if you're content just to help us find the man we're seeking, then there's no harm.

HOLMES: That is just how it does stand. Now perhaps we may have a clear account from you own lips. My friend here knows none of the details yet.

WATSON: Quite so!

JOHN GARRIDEB: Does he need to?

HOLMES: We usually work together.

JOHN GARRIDEB: Well – O.K. Dr. Watson, if you came from Kansas you wouldn't need me to tell you who Alexander Hamilton Garrideb was.

WATSON: Oh, really?

JOHN GARRIDEB: No sir! He made his pile in real estate in Chicago. But he spent it buying up land along the Arkansas River, west of Fort Dodge. It's grazing land and lumber land and arable land and mineralised land, and just every sort of land that brings dollars to the guy that owns it.

WATSON: I see.

JOHN GARRIDEB: Alexander Hamilton Garrideb had no kith or kin. But he took a kind of pride in the unusual name he had. I was in the law at Topeka, and he was tickled to death to meet another guy with that same name. 'Find me another, anywhere in the world,' said he, 'and you won't regret it.' I told him I was a busy man. I couldn't spend my life hiking round the world in search of Garridebs. 'None the less,' he said, 'that's just what you will do, if things pan out as I've planned them.'

HOLMES: What happened, Mr. Garrideb?

JOHN GARRIDEB: Alexander Hamilton Garrideb died – that's what happened, Mr. Holmes. He left a will behind him that was the queerest ever filed in the State of Kansas. His property was divided into three parts. I was to have one of them – on condition that I found two more Garridebs to share the remainder. We can't lay a finger on a cent of it until we all three stand in a row. But when we do it's five million dollars for each!

WATSON [*whistles*]: Remarkable!

JOHN GARRIDEB: Well, it was a chance in a lifetime. I let my legal practice slide and set forth looking for Garridebs.

WATSON: Can't say I blame you.

JOHN GARRIDEB: You can take my word for it, there isn't another one in the whole United States. I went through it with a fine-tooth comb. So I thought I'd try the old country. Sure enough, there was the name in the London telephone directory. I went after this Nathan Garrideb and explained the whole matter to him. But he's a lone man, like me.

HOLMES: With no relatives?

JOHN GARRIDEB: Some women, but no men. The will says three adult men. So there you are, Mr. Holmes. We still have a vacancy, and if you can help fill it we'll be very ready to pay your charges.

HOLMES: Well, Watson, I said it was a whimsical business, didn't I?

WATSON: That's the word for it. I should have thought your obvious course was to advertise in the agony columns of the newspapers, Mr. Garrideb.

JOHN GARRIDEB: Oh, I've done that. No replies.

HOLMES: Dear me! Well, it is certainly a most curious little problem. Yes, I may take a glance at it at my leisure.

JOHN GARRIDEB [*rising*]: I'd be mighty grateful, Mr. Holmes.

HOLMES: You'll let me know how you are progressing, Mr. Garrideb?

[HOLMES *and* WATSON *rise*]

JOHN GARRIDEB: Oh, sure, sure.

HOLMES: By the way, you come from Topeka, you say. I used to correspond with a gentleman there. He's dead now – old Dr. Lysander Starr. He was Mayor in 1890 or thereabouts.

JOHN GARRIDEB: Old Dr. Starr! His name is still honoured in Topeka, Mr. Holmes. Well, good day, gentlemen. I reckon you'll hear from me in a day or two.

HOLMES }
WATSON } Good day, Mr. Garrideb.

[*He exits.* HOLMES *returns to his chair, lapsing into deep thought.* WATSON *remains standing*]

WATSON[*chuckling*]: Well, Holmes – what a business! So you think that if I can lay hands on a Garrideb, these other two will pay a reward. It'd certainly help my wound pension! [*He rubs his leg*] Eh, Holmes? Holmes?

HOLMES [*back from thought*]: I beg your pardon, Watson?

WATSON: Oh, never mind. What do you think?

HOLMES: I'm wondering, Watson – just wondering what on earth could the man's object be in telling us such a rigmarole of lies.

WATSON: Lies!

HOLMES: I nearly asked him outright. There are times when a brutal frontal attack is the best policy. But I thought it better to let him believe he had fooled us.

WATSON: How on earth do you mean?

HOLMES: Here is a man with an English coat frayed at the elbow and trousers bagged at the knee with a year's wear – and yet by this document and his own account he's a provincial American not long in London. There have been no such advertisements in the agony columns. You know I never miss anything there.

WATSON: But he is from Topeka, evidently. He knew of your old friend, Dr. . . . whatsisname?

HOLMES: Lysander Starr? Well, *I* never knew such a gentleman.

WATSON: You didn't!

HOLMES: I invented him on the spur of the moment. So you see, Watson – touch this fellow where you would, he was false.

WATSON: You think he isn't even an American, then?

HOLMES: No, I wouldn't go so far as that. But he's worn his accent smooth with years of London.

WATSON: Then what's his game? What's the meaning of this search for Garridebs?

HOLMES: Whatever it is, it's worth our attention. Granting that the man's a rascal, he's certainly a complex and ingenious one. We must now find out if our other correspondent is a fraud also.

WATSON: Nathan Garrideb?

HOLMES: Exactly. [*Jumping up*] Come, Watson. I fancy we may well find him at home at this time of the evening.

[*They exit.* MRS. HUDSON *enters. She replaces* WATSON'S *glass on the tray, together with the letter and envelope, turns the lamp lower and exits, carrying the tray. The stage remains empty for a few moments*]

SCENE TWO

[*The stage as before.* MRS. SAUNDERS *enters from the side opposite to that used by* MRS. HUDSON. *She carries two or three learned-looking books. She places the books on the table, turns up the lamp, shifts the chairs a little more, then goes to the portrait of Queen Victoria, turning it back to front to reveal a picture of the Sphinx. We are now in* NATHAN GARRIDEB'S *study. As* MRS. SAUNDERS *completes these tasks,* NATHAN GARRIDEB *enters slowly, shuffling rather than walking, peering short-sightedly through his spectacles at an ancient vase he is holding*]

MRS. SAUNDERS: Ow, there you are, Mr. Garrideb!

NATHAN GARRIDEB [*peering at her*]: Eh? What? Oh, Mrs. Saunders!

MRS. SAUNDERS: Been looking for you all over the 'ouse, I 'ave. There's two gents to see you.

NATHAN GARRIDEB: Gents . . . Er, gentlemen? See me? Goodness gracious!

[*He resumes his scrutiny of the vase*]

MRS. SAUNDERS: Well, will I show 'em in, then?

NATHAN GARRIDEB: Eh? Show . . .? Ah, yes, yes. To be sure.

[MRS. SAUNDERS *exits, rolling her eyes despairingly at the audience as she goes.* GARRIDEB *is lost again in the study of his vase.* MRS. SAUNDERS *ushers in* HOLMES *and* WATSON *in street clothes*]

MRS. SAUNDERS: Mr. Sherlock 'olmes, Dr. Wilson.
WATSON: Watson.

[MRS. SAUNDERS *gives him a malevolent look and exits.* GARRIDEB *takes no notice of them. They exchange a glance.* WATSON *clears his throat noisily.* GARRIDEB *looks up, surprised*]

NATHAN GARRIDEB: Ah! Gentlemen! Mr. Holmes, wasn't it? And Dr. . . .?
WATSON [*with a sigh*]: Watson.
NATHAN GARRIDEB: To be sure! I wrote to you earlier today. [HOLMES *and* WATSON *exchange an amused glance*] Do sit down, gentlemen.

[HOLMES *takes one chair.* WATSON *is about to take the other when* GARRIDEB *alarms him by springing forward with a cry and picking something off the seat, to hold it aloft. It is a coin.* WATSON, *relieved, sits down*]

NATHAN GARRIDEB: There! I've been searching for that coin all day. Syracusan of the best period. They degenerated greatly towards the end, and some prefer the Alexandrian school. But I hold these supreme.

[*He puts the vase and the coin on the table and stands back to admire the former*]

You see my little interests in life, gentlemen. My doctor lectures me about never going out, never taking exercise. But why should I go anywhere, when I have so much to keep me here? I can assure you, the adequate cataloguing of my cabinets of fossils alone would take me a good three months.
HOLMES: But do you *never* go out, sir?
NATHAN GARRIDEB: Mm? Oh, now and again I drive down to the auction rooms. Otherwise, no. I very seldom leave these rooms. My researches are too

absorbing. But you can imagine, Mr. Holmes, what a terrific shock – pleasant, mind you, but terrific – it was for me when I heard of this unparalleled good fortune. It only needs one more Garrideb to complete the matter! And surely we can find one?

HOLMES: It is possible.

NATHAN GARRIDEB: I had heard that you handled strange cases, Mr. Holmes, and that was why I sent to you. Of course, this American gentleman is quite right. I should have taken his advice before doing so. But I acted for the best.

HOLMES: Mr. Garrideb, are you really anxious to acquire an estate in America?

NATHAN GARRIDEB: Certainly not, sir! But this gentleman has assured me that he will buy me out as soon as we have established our claim. Five million dollars was the sum named. There are a dozen specimens in the market at the present moment which would fill gaps in my collection, and which I am unable to purchase for want of a few hundred pounds. Just think what I could do with five million dollars!

WATSON: Quite understandable.

NATHAN GARRIDEB: But, forgive me, may I ask the purpose of your visit this evening, gentlemen?

HOLMES: Purely in order to make your acquaintance, Mr. Garrideb. There are a few questions I need to ask.

NATHAN GARRIDEB: I shall be happy to answer any there are.

[*He sits*]

HOLMES: This American gentleman – Mr. John Garrideb. I understand from your letter that up to this week you were unaware of his existence.

NATHAN GARRIDEB: That is so. He called last Tuesday.

HOLMES: Has he told you of our interview with him today?

NATHAN GARRIDEB: Yes, he came straight back to me. He had been very angry before. He seemed to think my writing to you was some reflection on his honour. But he was quite cheerful when he returned.

HOLMES: Did he suggest any course of action?

NATHAN GARRIDEB: He did not.

HOLMES: Has he had, or asked for, any money from you?

NATHAN GARRIDEB: Never.

HOLMES: You see no possible object he has in view?

NATHAN GARRIDEB: None, except what he states.

HOLMES [*thoughtfully*]: I see. Mr. Garrideb, have you any articles of great value in your collection?

NATHAN GARRIDEB: No, sir. I am not a rich man. It is a good collection, but not a very valuable one.

HOLMES: You have no fear of burglars?

NATHAN GARRIDEB: Not the least.

HOLMES: How long have you been in these rooms?

NATHAN GARRIDEB: Nearly five years.

[JOHN GARRIDEB *enters hastily*]

Oh! Mr. Garrideb! Do step in, sir.

JOHN GARRIDEB: Thank *you*, Mr. Garrideb.

[*He quickly approaches* NATHAN GARRIDEB, *waving a scrap of newspaper at him*]

Here we are! Here we are! Mr. Garrideb, my congratulations, sir!

NATHAN GARRIDEB: Congrat ...? Mr. Garrideb! You don't ... you don't say ...!

JOHN GARRIDEB: You're a rich man, Mr. Garrideb. We're both rich men!

NATHAN GARRIDEB: Oh!

JOHN GARRIDEB: Mr. Holmes, Dr. Watson – we can only say we're sorry we've troubled you unnecessarily.

WATSON: Really?

JOHN GARRIDEB: Here, Doctor. Read this. It's an advertisement from a newspaper in Birmingham. My agent there sent me it.

HOLMES: Birmingham Warwickshire, or Birmingham Alabama?

JOHN GARRIDEB: Warwickshire, or course! Right here in your own Midlands. Go on, Doctor – read it!

[WATSON *takes the paper*]

WATSON [*reads*]: 'Howard Garrideb ...' Good heavens! 'Howard Garrideb, Constructor of Agricultural Machinery. Binders, reapers, steam and hand plows ...' Hah! Spelt P-L-O-W-S! These provincial newspapers!

NATHAN GARRIDEB: Oh, do go on, sir!

WATSON: Sorry! [*Reads*] '... plows, drills, harrows, farmers' carts, buckboards ...' Buckboards? '... and all other appliances. Estimates for Artesian Wells. Apply Grosvenor Buildings, Aston.'

NATHAN GARRIDEB: Glorious! Wonderful! The third Garrideb!

JOHN GARRIDEB: You said it! And now we must hustle. I've written to this guy and told him you'll be at his office tomorrow afternoon at four.

NATHAN GARRIDEB: You – you want *me* to see him?

JOHN GARRIDEB: That's the idea. Don't you agree, Mr. Holmes? Here am I, a wandering Yank with a wonderful tale. Why should be believe me? But a Britisher with solid references ... He's bound to take notice of you, Mr. Garrideb. Mind, I wish I could go along with you, but I have a pretty busy day ahead tomorrow.

NATHAN GARRIDEB: But ... but I haven't made such a journey for years!

JOHN GARRIDEB: Aw, it's nothing, Mr. Garrideb. I've figured out your connections for you. You leave at twelve and you can be back here the same night.

NATHAN GARRIDEB: But . . .

JOHN GARRIDEB: All you have to do is see this guy, explain the matter, and get an affidavit of his existence. Gee whiz! Here I've come, all the way from the States! You surely don't figure a hundred miles or so too much trouble for your share?

HOLMES: I quite agree, Mr. Garrideb. I think that what Mr. John Garrideb says is quite true.

JOHN GARRIDEB: You see!

NATHAN GARRIDEB [*disconsolately*]: Well . . . If you insist, I shall go. It is certainly hard for me to refuse you any request, sir, considering the hope you have brought into my life.

HOLMES: Then that is agreed. No doubt you will let me have a report as soon as you can? I must complete my records of the case, you understand?

JOHN GARRIDEB: Sure, sure. I'll see to that. And now, I'll have to get on. I'll call tomorrow and see you off to Birmingham, Mr. Garrideb. [*Going*] Good night, gentlemen. Good night, Mr. Garrideb.

[*He exits*]

NATHAN GARRIDEB: Good night, Mr. Garrideb. [*Sighs*] Ah, dear me! Dear me!

HOLMES: Mr. Garrideb, I should very much appreciate a glance over your collection. In my profession all sorts of odd knowledge comes in useful.

NATHAN GARRIDEB [*brightening*]: Ah! I'd always heard you were a very intelligent man, Mr. Holmes. I could show you it now, if you have the time?

HOLMES: Unfortunately, no. But supposing I should be able to look in tomorrow while you are away, I presume there would be no objection to my looking round?

NATHAN GARRIDEB: None at all, my dear sir. Most welcome! Mrs. Saunders is in the basement up to four o'clock. I will say a word to her, and she will be ready to let you in.

HOLMES: Capital! [*He moves as if to go, but pauses*] Oh, by the way – who is your house agent?

NATHAN GARRIDEB: My . . .? Oh, I rent these rooms from, let me see, Holloway and Steele, in the Edgware Road. But if I may ask . . .?

HOLMES: No matter, my dear Mr. Garrideb. No matter at all. Come along, Watson.

WATSON: Good evening, Mr. Garrideb.

NATHAN GARRIDEB [*puzzled*]: Good . . . good evening, gentlemen.

[HOLMES *and* WATSON *exit.* GARRIDEB *stares after them for a moment, then shrugs, picks up the vase and wanders off examining it in the direction from which he first entered.* MRS. SAUNDERS *enters from the opposite side, flicking at things with a feather mop. She takes down the hanging picture, picks up the books from the table, and exits opposite. The stage remains empty for a few moments*]

SCENE THREE

[*The stage as before.* MR. HOLLOWAY'S CLERK *enters, carrying a ledger and a poster about a property for sale and bearing the name of* HOLLOWAY AND STEELE. *He places the ledger and poster on the table, then moves the chairs so that the table is set like a desk, with one chair at one side of it and two at the other. Then he hangs the poster from the picture hook and has just completed doing so when* HOLMES *and* WATSON *enter from the opposite side. They still wear street clothes, and* WATSON *carries a walking-cane. The* CLERK *sketches a bow*]

CLERK: Good morning, gentlemen. Mr. Holmes? Dr. Watson?

WATSON: The same.

CLERK: Mr. Holloway received your message for an appointment and will be most pleased to see you. If you'll just take a seat . . .?

[*He gestures towards the two chairs.* HOLMES *and* WATSON *sit*]

I'll tell him you're here and he'll be out directly, I'm sure.

WATSON: Thank you.

[*The* CLERK *exits with another little bow.* WATSON *waits until he has gone*]

Holmes, will you kindly stop being so secretive and tell me why it's necessary to come to these estate agents?

HOLMES: For a little information, that is all. Now that our little problem is drawing to a close . . .

WATSON: Drawing to a close!

HOLMES: Surely you've outlined the solution in your own mind?

WATSON: I can't make head nor tail of it!

HOLMES: Oh, the head is clear enough. We should see the tail before today is out.

WATSON: Holmes, what *are* you talking about?

HOLMES [*sighing*]: What struck you as curious about that advertisement our American friend produced?

WATSON: The advertisement? Why, only that spelling mistake. [*Chuckles*] P-L-O-W for plough!

HOLMES: Nothing else?

WATSON: No. Well . . .

HOLMES: Ah!

WATSON: There was a word new to me. Buckboard.

HOLMES: Watson, you improve all the time. A buckboard is a waggon seat – in America. P-L-O-W is bad English – but good American.

WATSON: I see!

HOLMES: And Artesian Wells, which were also mentioned, are commoner in America than with us. In other words, it was a typical American advertisement, but purporting to be from an English firm.

WATSON: Then – you mean to suggest this American lawyer had it printed himself?

HOLMES: What else do you make of it?

WATSON: But why?

HOLMES: There are other possibilities, of course. But he wanted to get that good old fossil up to Birmingham at all costs – that is clear.

WATSON: But you urged him to go!

HOLMES: I might have told him he was on a wild-goose chase; but on second thoughts it seemed better to clear the stage by letting him go. You see, Watson . . .

[*He breaks off suddenly and nudges* WATSON *as* HOLLOWAY *enters briskly, to take his seat at the other side of the desk*]

HOLLOWAY: Mr. Holmes, Dr. Watson? *Too* pleased to be of service, gentlemen. Some enquiry about a house in Little Ryder Street, I understand?

HOLMES: Number one hundred and thirty-six.

HOLLOWAY: Ah, I know it well. Very well. It has been on our books for many years.

[*He taps the ledger*]

HOLMES: A friend of mine, Mr. Garrideb, is your tenant.

HOLLOWAY: Quite so, quite so.

HOLMES [*with a glance at* WATSON]: He, er, suggested we call on you in our efforts to find out whether an acquaintance of mine – whose name I have unfortunately forgotten – lived there before Mr. Garrideb himself. If you could possibly be so kind . . .?

HOLLOWAY: Think nothing of it, sir.

[*He opens the ledger and begins riffling through the pages*]

Let me see, Mr. Garrideb has been there five years. Now . . .

[*He pauses at a page*]

Ah, but of course! The house was empty before that.

HOLMES: Empty!

HOLLOWAY: For about a year, that is – while we were trying to trace the previous tenant. Did a flit, as we say. [*Suspiciously*] Not *your* friend, I trust, Mr. Holmes?

HOLMES [*with mock indignation*]: Really, sir!

HOLLOWAY: Dear me, sir, no offence intended, I'm sure!

[*He begins to turn more pages*]

HOLMES [*casually*]: I suppose you suffer a good many cases of that sort of thing in your business, Mr. Holloway? People leaving owing you money?

HOLLOWAY: All too many, sir, all too many. There one day, gone the next, and never seen again. Mind you, this particular person was paid up six months in advance, so we'd no cause to complain at first. But then the arrears began mounting and, well, we just had to re-let.

WATSON: Disgraceful! Sheer lack of consideration!

HOLMES: Do you know, Mr. Holloway, although I'm almost ashamed to admit it, what you are saying does remind me somehow of this acquaintance of mine – oh, a very slight acquaintance, I assure you. Irresponsible, inclined to be haphazard . . .

HOLLOWAY: Well, Mr. Holmes, if you run across him again, you might do *us* the favour of letting us know.

HOLMES: With pleasure. Now, let me try to remember . . . about medium height with light coloured hair?

HOLLOWAY: Oh, no. Tall. Very dark features. And a beard. I remember him well.

HOLMES: Ah! And I think I begin to do so too, from your description. Now, if I could just catch his name . . .

[*He bangs his forehead with his fist*]

HOLLOWAY: Waldron. Mr. Joseph Waldron.

HOLMES: Of course!

[*He leaps to his feet.* WATSON *and* HOLLOWAY *rise more slowly*]

Mr. Holloway, I really am obliged to you. Clearly I cannot trace this person, and my reason for wishing to do so was, in any case, only slight. But you have shown me every courtesy, and if I hear further of him you may count upon me to let you know. My dear Watson . . .

WATSON [*bewildered*]: Yes, Holmes?

HOLMES: We are taking up this gentleman's valuable time. [*To* HOLLOWAY] Good-day, sir, and thank you.

[*He marches off.* WATSON *hesitates, then nods to* HOLLOWAY *and follows.* HOLLOWAY *bows deeply, closes the ledger and turns to go. He catches sight of the poster*]

HOLLOWAY [*calling*]: Mr. Jenkins!

HOLLOWAY'S CLERK [*off-stage*): Sir?

[*He appears*]

HOLLOWAY [*pointing to the poster*]: It's sold.

[*He marches off with the ledger. The* CLERK *takes down the poster and walks off after him. The stage remains empty for a few moments*]

SCENE FOUR

[*The stage as before.* A POLICE CONSTABLE *enters, carrying a rolled poster, which he proceeds to hang from the picture-hook. It comprises many head-and-shoulders portraits of men. He stands, hands behind his back, beside the poster.* HOLMES, WATSON *and* INSPECTOR LESTRADE *enter*]

LESTRADE: There's just a few more, Mr. Holmes, and then I'm afraid the searching gets harder. Ah, Constable, you've found 'em, then.

CONSTABLE [*nodding towards the poster*]: Yessir.

HOLMES: Inspector Lestrade, I'm deeply indebted. It isn't the first time this Rogues' Gallery of yours has helped me.

[*He goes and examines the portraits on the poster*]

LESTRADE: You're welcome any time.

[HOLMES *stabs his finger suddenly at one of the portraits*]

HOLMES: Ah!

LESTRADE: Got him, have you?

HOLMES: See, Watson.

WATSON: Great heavens! John Garrideb!

LESTRADE: Garrideb? That's 'Killer' Evans! Alias Morecroft. Real name, James Winter.

HOLMES: Excellent! Any more details?

LESTRADE: Suppose you tell me first what you want with him? And what's all this talk about a Garrideb, or something?

HOLMES: Oh, nothing. Nothing at all. Just a course of enquiry I've chosen to pursue.

LESTRADE: You wouldn't hold anything back?

HOLMES: My dear Lestrade!

LESTRADE [*chuckling*]: Oh, well, I should know better than to ask. Now, let's see – 'Killer' Evans. Yes. [*Enumerating on his fingers*] Native of Chicago. Known to have shot three men in the States, but got out of prison through political influence. Came to London – let's see, 1893. Shot a man over cards in a nightclub in the Waterloo Road in January '95. Got manslaughter. Came out last year and hasn't been in trouble since.

WATSON: A dangerous customer, Inspector.

LESTRADE: Very. Carries arms and ready to use 'em.

HOLMES: Hm! This man he shot in London – who was he?

LESTRADE: Prescott. Roger Prescott. Came from Chicago, too. Quite a name there as a forger and counterfeiter.

HOLMES: Have you his picture?

LESTRADE: Once they're dead we file 'em away. Take weeks to find.

HOLMES: Can you remember what he looked like?

LESTRADE: Tall chap. Very dark features – and a beard.

HOLMES: Ah!

LESTRADE: Here! You *do* know something, Mr. Holmes!

HOLMES: No, no. Lestrade, you've been as helpful as ever. I will say this for Scotland Yard – there may be an occasional want of imagination, but for thoroughness and method you lead the world.

[*The* CONSTABLE *is trying not to laugh*]

LESTRADE: Now, then, Mr. Holmes!

[*He sees the* CONSTABLE *grinning and glares at him.* LESTRADE *turns to exit, jerking his thumb at the* CONSTABLE *who takes down the poster*]

You can find you own way out, gentlemen?

HOLMES: Thank you, Lestrade.

WATSON: Good-day, Inspector.

[LESTRADE *exits, followed by the* CONSTABLE]

WATSON: So, Holmes, our American lawyer is none other than 'Killer' Evans!

HOLMES: With another alias to add to his list – John Garrideb. Well, the picture begins to define itself now. Our client, as he told us, has lived in that house for five years. It was empty for a year before that, because the previous tenant, a man named Waldron, had unaccountably disappeared. Waldron was a tall, bearded man with very dark features. So was Prescott, the man 'Killer' Evans shot in 1895, which would be about the time Waldron disappeared.

WATSON: Then – you think that Prescott and Waldron were the same man?

HOLMES: As a working hypothesis, I think we may take it that Prescott, the American forger and counterfeiter, used to live in the very rooms which our innocent friend Nathan Garrideb now devotes to his museum. And 'Killer' Evans, alias John Garrideb, is clearly interested in those rooms.

WATSON: And our next move?

HOLMES? We must go there this afternoon, while our friend is absent in Birmingham. In the meantime, I should devote an hour to cleaning your service revolver. [*They move towards the exit*] If our Wild West friend tries to live up to his nickname, we must be ready for him.

[*They exit. The stage remains empty for a few moments*]

SCENE FIVE

[*The stage as before.* MRS. SAUNDERS *enters, carrying the picture of the Sphinx and polishing its glass with a duster. She hangs it from the hook and straightens it. Then she rearranges the furniture, flicking at it with her duster. There is a knock at the door at the opposite side to that from which she entered. She goes to answer it, disappears from sight for a moment, then re-enters with* HOLMES *and* WATSON]

MRS. SAUNDERS: Mr. Garrideb left word you would be calling, sir. Said you was to look at anything you wanted.

HOLMES: Thank you, Mrs. Saunders.

[*He produces a coin*]

I am sure you have more than enough work calling you.

MRS. SAUNDERS [*with a little bob*]: Thank *you*, sir. You've only to ring if you want anything. I'll be in the basement.

WATSON: Thank you.

[*She bobs again and exits, with a last flick of her duster at a chair as she goes.* WATSON *runs his finger along a chair back, looks distastefully at the dust on it and holds it up to* HOLMES]

HOLMES: Never mind, my dear fellow. A more conscientious servant would not have left us alone – and I fancy our American friend will be coming visiting shortly. We do not want other company.

WATSON: What shall we do when he comes?

[HOLMES *glances round, looking for a place of concealment, then points to one of the exits*]

That alcove will do. There's room in it for us both.

WATSON: What makes you think he'll come?

HOLMES: He wanted to get Nathan Garrideb out of these rooms – that is very clear. As the old fellow never goes out of his own accord, it took some planning to arrange it.

WATSON: Then the whole of this Garrideb invention was apparently for no other end?

HOLMES: I must say there is a certain devilish ingenuity about it.

WATSON: Lucky for him the rooms are tenanted by someone with such an outlandish name.

HOLMES: That undoubtedly gave him his opening. But he wove his plot with remarkable cunning.

WATSON: What's he after, then?

HOLMES: That is what we are here to find out. As far as I can see, it has nothing at all to do with Nathan Garrideb. It is something connected with the man who was shot – Prescott. There's some guilty secret in this room, or so I read it.

WATSON: Maybe there's something valuable in the collection. Something the old man doesn't realise he owns.

HOLMES: No. The fact that Roger Prescott, of evil memory, once lived in these rooms points to some deeper reason than that. [*Lower*] Listen!

[*They listen*]

He's at the door! Quickly!

[*They hasten into the alcove.* WATSON *remains peeping out and draws his revolver.* JOHN GARRIDEB *enters cautiously from the opposite side.*

After a glance round he goes straight to the piece of matting and throws it aside. He takes out a knife and works for some moments, as though prising up the small trapdoor. It gives, and he lays the knife aside. He lifts the trapdoor and kneels, staring down. WATSON *comes stealthily forward, brandishing the revolver, followed by* HOLMES]

HOLMES: You have found what you are seeking, I trust, Mr. Garrideb?

JOHN GARRIDEB: Holmes!

[*He rises slowly, his hand going cautiously to his pocket*]

Well, well! I guess you've been one too many for me. Saw through my game, eh, and played me for a sucker from the first. Well, sir, I sure hand it to you, but ...

[*He whips out a revolver.* HOLMES *leaps forward and brings* JOHN GARRIDEB *to the floor, but the gun fires as he falls and* WATSON *drops his own revolver as he crumples to the ground.* HOLMES *strikes* GARRIDEB, *who goes still*]

HOLMES: Watson!

WATSON [*groans*].

HOLMES: Watson! Tell me you're not hurt, my dear old friend.

WATSON: I ... I don't think it's much, Holmes. My calf ...

[HOLMES *pounces on* WATSON'S *trouser leg, pulling it up to examine the wound. He pulls out a vast handkerchief and quickly dresses it*]

HOLMES: You'll live, Watson. A mere scratch.

WATSON [*sitting up rather quickly*]: Oh!

HOLMES [*hard*]: By the Lord Harry, it's as well for that devil there. If he'd killed you he would never have left this room alive.

[WATSON *struggles to rise.* HOLMES *tries to restrain him, but* WATSON *insists. He tests his leg and finds he can stand perfectly well*]

WATSON: Quite all right, Holmes. Just went down with the shock.

HOLMES: Then come along, my dear fellow, and let us see what it is beneath the floorboards that so interested this scoundrel.

[*They lift the trap.* WATSON *peers down*]

WATSON: A cellar. Machinery . . . bottles . . . paper . . .

HOLMES: The late Prescott's outfit.

[JOHN GARRIDEB *groans and raises himself on to an elbow*]

JOHN GARRIDEB: The greatest forger and counterfeiter England ever saw. No man could tell a Prescott from a Bank of England.

WATSON: You killed him.

JOHN GARRIDEB: Yes, and got five years for it. Five years, when I should by rights have had a medal the size of a soup plate. If I hadn't fixed him he'd have flooded London with his fake notes. But I got five years – the only man who knew where he made them.

HOLMES: You served your sentence and waited to get back here.

JOHN GARRIDEB: And then what? I find this crazy old boob of a collector squatting right on top of a fortune, and never going out. I had to shift him somehow. You may think my scheme was far-fetched, but how *do* you shift a guy out of his own home?

WATSON: With your record, Evans, I am surprised you didn't use a more direct method.

[JOHN GARRIDEB *gets up and spreads his open hands*]

JOHN GARRIDEB: No, sir. I'm a soft-hearted sucker that can't start shooting unless the other guy has a gun. If you hadn't waved yours at me just now I'd have given up like a lamb. I . . . I'm sorry, Doctor.

WATSON: Well . . . it was only a scratch.

JOHN GARRIDEB: Swell. But say, Mr. Holmes, what have I done wrong, anyways? I've not used this plant. I never hurt the old geezer. What do you get me on?

HOLMES [*grimly*]: Attempted murder of my greatest friend will do for the moment.

[*He gives* JOHN GARRIDEB *a long, severe stare; then, suddenly, he smiles*]

But who knows – when Scotland Yard hear that you have led them to a fortune in counterfeit money, they may even give you that medal you seek.

[*Curtain begins to fall*]

You can wear it on your prison uniform.

THE REIGATE SQUIRES

SCENE I: The morning room of Colonel Hayter's house
SCENE II: Outside Cunningham's house
SCENE III: Cunningham's parlour

Characters in order of appearance:

COLONEL HAYTER: Sixties. Former army officer and friend of Watson.

DR. WATSON

SHERLOCK HOLMES

BLAKE: Colonel Hayter's butler.

INSPECTOR FORRESTER: Surrey Constabulary. 'A smart, keen-faced young fellow.'

TWO CONSTABLES

WILLIAM KIRWAN: A corpse.

CUNNINGHAM, J.P.: Elderly, strong.

ALEC CUNNINGHAM: His son. 'A dashing young fellow.'

THE REIGATE SQUIRES

SCENE ONE

[*The morning room of* COLONEL HAYTER'S *country house near Reigate. One or two chairs, a small table, a decanter and sherry glasses.* HAYTER *is pouring sherry for* WATSON *and himself. They raise their glasses to one another*]

HAYTER: Great pleasure to see you again, Watson, old chap.
WATSON: My dear Hayter, delighted.

[*They drink*]

Ah!
HAYTER: Good few years since Afghanistan, what?
WATSON: Six or seven. I keep forgetting, until the weather turns damp and the old wound reminds me.
HAYTER: Hah! Know what you mean. Play the very deuce in a cold snap, don't they?

[*He rubs his hip meaningfully*]

Still, it would have been a confounded sight worse without a surgeon like you on hand, Watson. Lucky I got mine before you stopped yours, eh?

[*They laugh*]

You've been having an interesting enough time since, by all accounts.
WATSON [*nodding*]: I don't mind admitting, Hayter, I was pretty well on my beam ends after they let me out of

hospital. Pension going straight into my bookie's pocket each week: no capital to buy a decent practice.

HAYTER: Too bad! Too bad!

WATSON: Then, quite by chance, I met a young chap who'd been a dresser under me at Bart's. Told him I was looking for cheap lodgings somewhere, and he mentioned this fellow he knew who wanted someone to go halves in a suite of rooms in Baker Street.

HAYTER: Well, well, well! And that's how you met Sherlock Holmes! Remarkable thing, coincidence!

[*He pours more sherry*]

WATSON: Mind you, I didn't know whether I could stick it at first. If there's an untidier man in London, I'd hate to meet him. Stuff all over the place! Books, papers, chemical experiments going on. He keeps cigars in the coal scuttle, his tobacco in an old slipper. He even sticks his letters and bills to the mantelpiece with a jack-knife . . .

[HAYTER *is laughing heartily*]

Strange people calling at all hours of the day and night . . .

HAYTER: Oh, my word!

WATSON: And what with his fiddle-playing, and his filthy pipe, and never being there for meals when they're ready, I reckon he must be about the worst tenant in London into the bargain. But our Mrs. Hudson worships him.

HAYTER: Shouldn't be surprised if you do, too, Watson.

WATSON: Well . . . [*He grins, but then looks more serious*] But you see what's happened now? Time and again I've warned him he couldn't go on living like that. He's never listened to me, and now he's paying the penalty.

[HAYTER *glances beyond* WATSON *and clears his throat warningly*]

HAYTER [*low*]: Here he comes.

WATSON: Oh, don't worry about that. I don't mince words about what I think of his goings-on. At least this breakdown might bring him to his senses.

[HOLMES *enters. He wears a dressing-gown over his clothes and his feet are slippered. He is pale and walks slowly, much pulled-down by illness*]

HAYTER [*going to him*]: Good morning, Mr. Holmes. Trust you slept well. Breakfast to your taste. Everything. Eh?

HOLMES [*shakes hands with him*]: Your arrangements are admirable, Colonel Hayter. It was . . . most kind of you to invite me here for a little rest.

[HAYTER *fusses him into a chair.* HOLMES *sinks down thankfully*]

HAYTER: My pleasure entirely, me dear chap. Thought I was just inviting my old Army friend here, but I'm delighted and honoured to entertain you as well. And you've to stay just as long as your doctor orders.

[*He nods at* WATSON, *who gives him a little bow*]

HOLMES: I don't mind admitting this has left me feeling a trifle knocked up.

WATSON [*snorts*]: Knocked up! Complete breakdown, you mean. [*He turns to* HAYTER] He'd been working fifteen hours a day for two months on this Netherlands–Sumatra case. He succeeded where the police of three continents failed. Telegrams of congratulation pouring in by the bucketful, and then he collapses completely – and he says he's a bit 'knocked up'!

HOLMES: Well, it's all a thing of the past for me now.

Springtime in Surrey and Colonel Hayter's hospitality are what matter for the present.

HAYTER [*laughs*]: Let's hope you won't be disturbed by any more of the fun we've been having here lately.

HOLMES: Fun?

[WATSON, *out of* HOLMES'S *sight, makes a cautionary gesture to* HAYTER]

HAYTER: Oh! Ah ... [*Clears his throat*] Nothing, really. Just a bit of nonsense been going on. Nothing at all, what?

HOLMES [*less languidly*]: You intrigue me, Colonel.

HAYTER: Well ... dash it, there's nothing to it really. Old Acton, one of our local squires, had his house broken into the other day. [*Laughs*] Matter of fact, it'll make you laugh. Never guess what they got away with. [*Telling the items off on his fingers*] Two plated candlesticks, ivory letter-weight, small oak barometer, ball of twine, and ... ah, yes – volume of Pope's Homer.

HOLMES [*sinking back*]: Well, the county police ought to be able to make something of it. Surely, it's obvious that ...

WATSON: Now, now, Holmes! You're here for a rest, remember?

HOLMES [*sighs*]: Oh, dear me, Watson. Well, I suppose I've got to do what *you* tell *me*, for a change.

HAYTER: That's right, Holmes. Had this treatment from him on the Frontier, you know. Regular martinet, this Watson.

[BLAKE *enters, agitated*]

BLAKE: Beg pardon, sir.

HAYTER: Yes, Blake? [*Peering at him*] Something the matter?

BLAKE: At the Cunninghams', sir ...

HAYTER: Eh? Not another burglary?

BLAKE: Murder, sir!

WATSON: Great heavens!

[HOLMES *sits up with interest*]

HAYTER: By Jove! Who? The J.P. or his son?

BLAKE: Neither, sir. It was William, the coachman. Shot through the 'eart.

HAYTER: Who shot him?

BLAKE: Oh, it was a burglar, sir. Got clean away. He'd just forced the pantry window, they say, when William disturbed him. Shot him dead and made off.

HAYTER: When was this, Blake?

BLAKE: Last night, sir. Somewhere about twelve.

HAYTER: Hm! Bad business. All right, Blake.

BLAKE [*going*]: Very good, sir.

[*He exits*]

HAYTER: Poor old Cunningham! Our leading squire about here. He'll be cut up about this, you know. The man had been in his service for years.

WATSON: Might be one of the same chaps who broke into the other place.

HAYTER: I fancy it's some local, myself. Acton's and Cunningham's are just the places he would go for. Largest in these parts.

HOLMES: And the richest?

HAYTER: Well, they ought to be. But they've had a lot of blood sucked out of them in recent years.

WATSON: How's that?

HAYTER: They've had a lawsuit dragging on for no end of time. Old Acton has some claim on half of Cunningham's estate. The lawyers have been at it with both hands.

HOLMES: Well, if it's a local man there shouldn't be much difficulty in running him down.

[BLAKE *enters*]

BLAKE: Inspector Forrester, sir.

HAYTER [*calling*]: Come in, Inspector.

[FORRESTER *enters.* BLAKE *exits*]

FORRESTER: Good morning, Colonel Hayter. I hope I don't intrude, sir, but we hear that Mr. Holmes of Baker Street is here.

HAYTER [*indicating him*]: There he is, Inspector. And this is Dr. Watson.

WATSON: How d'ye do?

[*They shake hands*]

FORRESTER: Pleased to meet you, gentlemen. You've heard the news, I expect. We, er, wondered if we could ask you to step across, Mr. Holmes?

WATSON: Certainly not, Inspector. Mr. Holmes is recuperating – under *my orders.*

HOLMES [*laughs: brisker now*] The Fates are against you, Watson. We were chatting about the matter when you came in, Inspector. Perhaps you'd care to take a seat and let us have a few details?

[WATSON *rolls his eyes hopelessly at* HAYTER, *who grins*]

FORRESTER: Thank you, sir. [*Sitting*] Well, we had no clue in the Acton affair, but we've plenty to go on this time.

HOLMES: Oh?

FORRESTER: The man was seen.

HAYTER: Aha!

FORRESTER: When the alarm broke out, Mr. Cunningham had just got into bed, and Mr. Alec Cunningham – that's his son – was smoking a pipe in the parlour. They both heard William, the coachman, call for help, and Mr. Alec ran out in his dressing-gown. The back door was open, and he saw the two men wrestling together outside. One of them fired a shot, the other dropped to the ground, and the murderer was off across the garden hedge. Mr. Cunningham saw him, too, from his bedroom window, as he reached the road.

HAYTER: Couldn't young Alec catch him?

FORRESTER: He'd stopped to do what he could for William, so the fellow got clean away. Middle-sized man, dressed in some dark stuff – that's the description we've got.

HOLMES: Did William say anything before he died?

FORRESTER: Not a word. But one thing we did get was this.

[*He fumbles in his waistcoat and produces a fragment of paper*]

[*Holding it up*] Seems to be a fragment of paper torn from a larger sheet. It was between the dead man's finger and thumb.

[*He gives it to* HOLMES, *who examines it keenly*]

HAYTER: So either the other chap tore the rest of the paper out of William's hand – or William tore this bit from a sheet the other chap was holding. Can't see what either of them was doing waving sheets of paper about.

FORRESTER: If you look at the words, though, it reads as if it's been some sort of appointment.

HOLMES [*reading*]: '... at quarter to twelve ...' Then down here it says 'learn what ...' Hm! This writing is of extraordinary interest. These are much deeper waters than I'd thought.

FORRESTER: How's that, Mr. Holmes? Do you reckon there was some sort of understanding between William and the burglar? William was to let him in, but they had a quarrel instead?

HOLMES: It's not entirely impossible. But this writing ... [*He peers intently at the paper*] No ... [*Eagerly*] There's something about it that fascinates me extremely. Colonel, if you'll excuse me I'll leave Watson with you and step round with the Inspector to put one or two little fancies of mine to the test.

[HOLMES *almost springs to his feet in his eagerness, handing the paper back to* FORRESTER]

WATSON: Holmes, you'll do nothing of the sort! I . . . I forbid you.

HOLMES: Never fear, Watson. I feel suddenly better. But I promise to deliver myself up to you in half an hour precisely.

WATSON: Well . . .

HOLMES [*mischievously*]: At Mr. Cunningham's door. You too, if you wish, Colonel.

[HOLMES *takes* FORRESTER *by the arm and pilots him swiftly from the room.* WATSON *steps forward, raising a hand in protest, but can only turn and shrug helplessly at* HAYTER, *who laughs and pours them another drink*]

HAYTER: Now, me dear chap, I see *exactly* what you mean.

[HAYTER *hands* WATSON *his glass and raises his own to him as the curtain falls*]

SCENE TWO

[*Outside Cunningham's house. This can be played in front of the curtain.* HOLMES *and* FORRESTER *enter R.* HOLMES *is now dressed in ulster and deerstalker and is puffing his pipe, peering about him intently. From L two* CONSTABLES *enter, carrying the draped body of* WILLIAM *on a stretcher.* FORRESTER *motions them to put it down. They do so and retreat a few paces to stand respectfully at ease*]

FORRESTER: Here we are, sir. Sorry you couldn't see it *in situ*, but it had been moved before I got here.

[HOLMES *kneels and turns back the sheet, examining the body keenly in the region of the heart*]

HOLMES: Undoubtedly killed by a single revolver bullet.

[*He takes out his magnifying glass and looks intently at the chest*]

Fired from at least four yards away.

[*He looks up at* FORRESTER]

FORRESTER: How's that, sir?

HOLMES: No powder-blackening on the clothing.

[FORRESTER *scratches his head.* HOLMES *replaces the sheet and straightens up*]

Inspector, will you show me the spot where the murderer escaped over the hedge?

[FORRESTER *indicates the extreme R of the stage*]

FORRESTER: Just over here, sir. The Cunninghams both pointed it out exactly.

[HOLMES *moves to where he has indicated and bends, hands on knees, to scrutinise the ground*]

HOLMES: Hm! One or two boot-marks . . . Let me see your soles, please.

[FORRESTER *raises one of his boot-soles for inspection.* HOLMES *nods*]

I expected as much. Otherwise . . . nothing.

[*He straightens up and stands staring down at the ground, puffing his pipe thoughtfully*]

FORRESTER: What do you make of it, Mr. Holmes?

[*They move back to mid-stage*]

HOLMES: Inspector, may I see that piece of paper again?

FORRESTER: Certainly, sir. [*He hands it to* HOLMES]

HOLMES [*after a moment*]: I think we're both agreed that the finding of this in the dead man's hand is of extreme importance.

FORRESTER: Well, it *has* got 'quarter to twelve' written on it – and that's almost the very moment he was killed.

HOLMES: Precisely. Whoever wrote that note was the man who brought William out of his bed at that hour. [*He holds up the torn fragment*] But where is the rest of this sheet of paper?

FORRESTER: I searched every inch for it.

HOLMES: It was torn out of the dead man's hand. Why was someone so anxious to get possession of it?

FORRESTER: Maybe it incriminated him.

HOLMES: Just so, Inspector. And what would he do with it, having got it? He would most likely thrust it into his pocket, never noticing that a corner had been left in the grip of the corpse.

[*He puts the paper slowly into his pocket, as though it is an automatic movement*]

FORRESTER: Very possible, Mr. Holmes.

HOLMES: Now, the man who wrote it wouldn't have written it at all if he could have delivered the message by word of mouth, would he?

FORRESTER: N-o.

HOLMES: So, who brought it? Or did it come through the post?

FORRESTER: Ah, that I can tell you, sir. We found out that William *did* get a letter by the afternoon post. No sign of the envelope anywhere, though.

HOLMES: Capital! Inspector Forrester, it's a pleasure to work with you. By the way, may I keep the piece of paper for the moment?

FORRESTER: If you wish, sir. Er, what about the body?

HOLMES: No, no. I fancy we have nothing more to learn from it.

[FORRESTER *gestures to the* CONSTABLES, *who pick up the stretcher and bear the body off R.* HAYTER *and* WATSON *enter R. at that moment, hastily removing their hats and standing respectfully as the body passes*]

Ah! Military promptitude.

WATSON: Holmes, how're you feeling?

HOLMES: Never better, my dear fellow.

HAYTER: Found out anything yet?

HOLMES: Yes, Colonel – that this crime is a very peculiar one. Perhaps our visit to the Cunninghams' may do something to make it less obscure.

HAYTER [*glancing past him to Stage L*]: Well, here they are.

[CUNNINGHAM *and* ALEC CUNNINGHAM *enter L.* HAYTER *moves to shake hands and introduce them*]

Cunningham, me dear chap – and Alec, me boy. So

sorry about all this. Terrible, terrible. Er, meet Mr. Sherlock Holmes and Dr. Watson.

[*Handshakes exchanged and* ad lib *greetings*]

CUNNINGHAM: Well, Mr. Holmes, we've heard of you – even in these parts.

ALEC: You don't mean to say the Inspector's called you in for anything so straightforward as this?

HOLMES: Hardly straightforward, I think.

CUNNINGHAM: Ah! Then you've found some sort of clue?

FORRESTER: In a way, sir. You see, there was a . . .

[*He breaks off as* HOLMES *gives a loud groan and faints at his feet*]

Mr. Holmes!

WATSON: Great heavens, I might have expected it. Quickly, please, help me with him into the house.

[*Between them they lift the unconscious* HOLMES *and carry him off L*]

SCENE THREE

[*The Cunninghams' parlour. A window (optional) is in the back wall. The room has an untidy air, with things littered about – walking sticks in a stand, a pair of boots, a chair with a deed-box and documents on it, etc. etc. It is a farmers' parlour with no woman to fuss over it. Slightly to R is a sofa or chaise-longue on which* HOLMES *lies, head back and eyes closed, his feet in the direction of stage L. Near the foot of the sofa is a small table on which stands a carafe of water. At L, an old dressing-gown hangs on a hat-stand or hook. Near to it is another small table on which are a lamp and some papers and a pencil. The* CUNNINGHAMS, FORRESTER *and* HAYTER *are ranged behind and around the sofa, looking down at* HOLMES. WATSON *hovers near his head with a glass of water ready.* HOLMES *groans and stirs*]

ALEC: He's coming to.

[WATSON *moves quickly to* HOLMES *and assists him as he struggles to sit up*]

WATSON: Easily, Holmes. Lie still for a bit.
HOLMES [*weakly*]: Watson?
WATSON: A sip of water?

[HOLMES *nods.* WATSON *holds the glass while he sips from it, then hands it to* FORRESTER, *who replaces it on the small table beside the decanter. They look on as* HOLMES *brushes his hand across his eyes, shakes his head to clear it, and, with* WATSON'S *aid, wriggles into a half-sitting position*]

No hurry, Holmes. Just take your time.

HAYTER: You, er, feeling all right now, old chap?

HOLMES [*with an effort*]: Thank you, Colonel. Gentlemen, I can't apologise enough.

CUNNINGHAM: Not at all.

HOLMES: These confounded nervous attacks. So suddenly...

CUNNINGHAM: Yes, yes. Dr. Watson's been telling us how ill you've been.

WATSON: *And* how you won't listen to commonsense, Holmes. The sooner you're back at Hayter's, and in bed, the better.

[HOLMES *nods weakly and shuts his eyes*]

CUNNINGHAM: Look here, I'll call my trap to take you back.

HOLMES: Perhaps in a little while.

WATSON: *Now*, Holmes.

HOLMES [*rather slyly*]: No – since I'm here, there is one little point I might as well verify.

[WATSON *and* HAYTER *exchange significant glances*]

I should like to ask Mr. Cunningham Junior what he was doing when he heard William call for help?

ALEC: I've told the Inspector – I was sitting smoking in here. I always do, last thing – wearing that disreputable old dressing-gown, I'm afraid. [*Pointing apologetically to it and grinning*]

HOLMES: By lamplight?

ALEC: Of course.

HOLMES: Doesn't it strike you as extraordinary that a burglar should break into a house when lights were on and the family might still be afoot?

CUNNINGHAM: Bit of a cool customer, perhaps.

HOLMES: Possibly. Mr. Cunningham, there is something I should like you to do.

CUNNINGHAM: Anything at all.

HOLMES: I should like you to offer a reward, which I will arrange to have published. If you have a pencil and paper, by any chance . . .?

[ALEC *picks them off the table with the lamp and hands them to* HOLMES]

Thank you.

[*He writes*]

Fifty pounds would be quite enough, I think.

[*He hands the paper to* CUNNINGHAM]

If you wouldn't mind reading it and signing it?

[CUNNINGHAM *reads*]

CUNNINGHAM: Yes, this is all right. But there's one little mistake. You begin [*reads*] 'Whereas, at about a quarter to one on Tuesday morning, an attempt was made . . . etcetera, etcetera.' Well, it was a quarter to twelve.

HOLMES: Dear me, of course you're right. I don't allow myself to make such elementary mistakes.

[*He offers the pencil to* CUNNINGHAM, *who takes it and alters the incorrect word*]

CUNNINGHAM: It's right now.

[*He hands the paper back to* HOLMES, *who glances at it and pockets it*]

HOLMES: Thank you. And now, Watson, I surrender to your charge.

WATSON: And about time too.

[WATSON *moves to assist* HOLMES, *who rises and leans slightly on his friend's arm. They walk slowly towards L. When they reach the table on which the decanter and glass stand,* HOLMES, *shielded from the others' view by* WATSON, *who does not see what he does, deliberately upsets it*]

HOLMES: Oh, Watson! What a clumsy fellow you are!

WATSON: I! Holmes . . .

HOLMES: Quickly – the carpet.

WATSON: Well, really, I . . .

[*He turns, pulling out his handkerchief to begin dabbing at the carpet. The others cluster round him, picking up the table and the broken glass. Unnoticed,* HOLMES *darts across to the dressing-gown and rummages in its pockets*]

CUNNINGHAM: Think nothing of it, Dr. Watson. Water won't do any harm.

[ALEC *glances up and sees* HOLMES. *He hesitates for a moment*]

WATSON: I really can't think how it happened . . .

[HOLMES *draws a piece of crumpled paper from the dressing-gown pocket*]

ALEC [*urgently*]: Father!

[CUNNINGHAM *looks up, follows his son's gaze and sees* HOLMES *beginning to straighten out the paper*]

CUNNINGHAM: Now, sir, this is going too far.

ALEC: Give me that.

[*He hurries to* HOLMES, *who is reading the paper, and tries to snatch it.* HOLMES *eludes him.* ALEC *grapples with him*]

HAYTER: I say, Alec! Cunningham!

CUNNINGHAM [*fiercely*]: Keep out of this!

[*He goes to help his son.* HOLMES *holds the paper high above his head, out of their reach, as they struggle with him*]

WATSON: Holmes . . .

HOLMES: Inspector – arrest these men.

FORRESTER: Arrest . . .?

HOLMES: For the murder of William, their coachman.

CUNNINGHAM: He's mad.

[WATSON, HAYTER *and* FORRESTER *have moved to try to separate them. There is a general mêlée*]

HAYTER: Another breakdown, Watson?

WATSON [*grimly, now struggling in earnest with* CUNNINGHAM]: I don't think so.

HOLMES: Quickly, Forrester – before they can snatch this paper. It's our vital evidence.

[FORRESTER *blows his whistle.* ALEC *breaks away and tugs a revolver from his pocket.* WATSON *leaps across to seize his arm and force it down. The revolver fires into the floor.* WATSON *wrenches* ALEC'S *arm and the weapon falls from his hand.* WATSON *puts his foot on it. The two* CONSTABLES *run in R and secure* ALEC *and* CUNNINGHAM, *indicated by* FORRESTER]

FORRESTER: Right. That's enough from you two.

HOLMES: Thank you, Inspector.

FORRESTER: Thank *you*, Mr. Holmes. I've seen enough to justify an arrest, though what your evidence is, I'll have to hear later. [*To the prisoners*] Come on, gentlemen.

[*The* CONSTABLES *urge them towards R*]

HOLMES: A moment. I should like Mr. Cunningham, or his son, to confirm one thing for me.

ALEC: You'll get nothing from me, Holmes.

HOLMES: I *am* right in thinking that William was blackmailing you both?

ALEC: Think what you like!

CUNNINGHAM: No, Alec. [*Wearily*] Yes, Mr. Holmes. You're right.

HOLMES: Thank you. That will be all.

[FORRESTER *signs to the* CONSTABLES *and follows them as they march the prisoners off R*]

HAYTER: Blackmail, Holmes? Blackmail? How on earth d'you know that?

[HOLMES *walks rather wearily to the chaise-longue and reclines on it again. He takes from his pocket the original fragment of paper and fits it to the larger one*]

HOLMES: Have a look at this.

[*They go round behind the chaise-longue and peer over his shoulder*]

Don't you observe something very revealing about it?

HAYTER: Can't say I do.

WATSON: Pretty irregular sort of handwriting.

HOLMES: Exactly, Watson. Of course, he is better up in my methods than you, Colonel. No, there cannot be the least doubt that this note was written by two persons.

WATSON: Two!

HOLMES: Doing alternate words.

HAYTER: By Jove, you're right! But what on earth for?

HOLMES: Obviously one mistrusted the other. The idea was that each of them should have an equal part in the business. Of the two, I should say that the ringleader was the man who wrote 'at' and 'to' and 'learn', etcetera.

HAYTER: However can you say that?

HOLMES: If you look closely, you'll see that those words were obviously written first, and blanks were left for the other writer to fill in. But they weren't always big enough. Look how the second man had to squeeze to get the word 'quarter' in between the 'at' and the 'to'.

WATSON: Bravo, Holmes!

HAYTER: Magnificent bit of deduction!

HOLMES: But very superficial. You may not know that the deduction of a man's age from his writing has been brought to considerable accuracy by experts. In this case, looking at the bold, strong hand of the one writer, and the rather broken-backed appearance of the other, we can say that the former was a young man and the latter was advanced in years, without being positively decrepit.

HAYTER: Well, I never heard anything to touch this. Did you read anything *else* in the handwriting?

HOLMES: Oh yes. There were at least twenty-three other deductions . . .

HAYTER: Twenty . . .!

HOLMES: But they would be of more interest to experts than to you, Colonel – except, perhaps, that some of them reveal quite clearly that the two writers were blood-relatives.

[HAYTER *and* WATSON *laugh*]

WATSON: How did you connect this with the Cunninghams, Holmes?

HOLMES: Oh, that came to my mind almost as soon as I saw the bullet wound in the dead man. There was no powder blackening on the clothes, so the shot must have been fired from at least four yards away. Yet Alec Cunningham had told the Inspector he saw William and his assailant at grips with one another at the time.

[HOLMES *gets up and prowls about*]

At the place where the Cunninghams had stated the murderer escaped across the hedge, the ground was soft enough to show impressions of the Inspector's boots – yet there were no traces of any others. I was not only sure that both the Cunninghams had lied, but that there had been no unknown man on the scene at all.

HAYTER: Then, you mean to say that one of them shot William?

HOLMES: Alec, at a guess.

HAYTER: But why?

HOLMES: I thought back at once to what you had told me about a burglary at the house of your friend Mr. Acton. What did you say was missing again?

HAYTER: Er, pair of candlesticks, ivory letter-weight, small barometer, ball of twine . . .

HOLMES: And a copy of Pope's Homer. A strange selection of loot, wouldn't you agree?

HAYTER: Hardly worth the risk.

HOLMES: Precisely. It seemed to be obvious that the burglars had been after something else, had failed to find it, so had swept a few things into their bag to make their search look like an ordinary burglary.

WATSON: Hayter, didn't you say there'd been a long lawsuit between Acton and the Cunninghams?

HAYTER: Going on for years.

WATSON: Then, it's my bet the Cunninghams did that burglary themselves. They were after some document without which Acton couldn't hope to win the case.

HOLMES: Capital, Watson! My reading entirely.

WATSON: Wait, Holmes. Their coachman, William, knew what they'd tried to do, and started blackmailing them. He'd be on his guard against them, so they concocted that note, as though it was from some stranger, to lure him into the grounds that night and murder him in a way no one could connect with them.

HOLMES: Magnificent! Watson, you're a credit to my training.

WATSON: Thank you. But I still don't see . . .

HOLMES: Dear me!

WATSON: I don't see how you knew where to find that other piece of paper that would prove all this. I mean, without that you could only assume they were guilty.

HOLMES: Quite true. I had to find the missing part of the note in the possession of one of them. I was certain that Alec must have torn it from the dead man's hand. He was wearing his dressing-gown at the time, I'd been told.

[*He takes the dressing-gown from its hook and fondles it*]

Ten to one he'd have thrust the paper unthinkingly into its pocket. I wanted badly to see that dressing-gown, but Inspector Forrester nearly ruined everything for me.

[FORRESTER *enters briskly R*]

FORRESTER: What's this, Mr. Holmes? Fair play, now!

HOLMES: When the Cunninghams joined us outside the house, you started to tell them about the one clue we'd found – that torn piece of paper in the dead man's hand. If you'd been allowed to finish, Alec would certainly remember the other piece in his dressing-gown pocket and hurry in here to destroy it. But, by the luckiest chance in the world, I, er, tumbled down in some sort of faint.

[*He tosses the dressing-gown to* FORRESTER *who catches it, astonished*]

FORRESTER: You . . . you mean to say you were bluffing!

WATSON [*laughing*]: Holmes, in all my years of practice I've seen plenty of fellows collapse at my feet, but I don't mind admitting you took me in.

HOLMES: Oh, it's an art I often find useful. Well, when I'd, er, recovered I managed by some little ingenuity to get old Cunningham to change the word 'one' to 'twelve' on that reward notice, so that I could compare his writing of 'twelve' with the 'twelve' in the original note.

HAYTER: And all this happened before our eyes. What a blind ass I've been!

HOLMES: Then, by contriving to upset that decanter . . .

WATSON: You see! I knew *I* hadn't knocked the blessed thing over!

HOLMES: . . . I managed to divert attention long enough to search the dressing-gown pockets and find what I wanted. [*Yawns*] Alec saw that the game would be up in a moment, hence his recourse to violence. [*Yawns*] Oh, dear me!

[*He goes back to the chaise-longue and stretches out on it*]

Watson, you should have reminded me that I'm an invalid.

[WATSON *rolls his eyes helplessly.* HOLMES *lays back his head and shuts his eyes*]

FORRESTER: Just a minute, Mr. Holmes. There's a lot of details I want to hear from you.

HOLMES [*eyes shut, yawning*]: Apply to Watson. He will embellish the narrative with far more colour than I should give it.

[WATSON *gives* HOLMES *a hard look, then takes the dressing-gown from* FORRESTER *and drapes it across* HOLMES'S *body, picking up the paper as he does so. He beckons* FORRESTER *over to L,* HAYTER *following, and shows him the paper*]

WATSON [*quietly*]: First of all, Inspector, have a look at this. Don't you observe something very revealing about the handwriting?

[FORRESTER *peers, then stares at* WATSON, *scratching his head. The curtain falls slowly*]

Now, to an expert, there can be no possible doubt that this note was written by two persons, doing alternate words. If you'll look closely it'll be quite obvious to you that one of them was elderly and one young, and which of them was the ringleader. You see how one left blanks for the other to fill in, and . . .

BLACK PETER

SCENE I: 221B Baker Street, *morning*

SCENE II: Capt. Peter Carey's 'cabin', *that afternoon and evening*

SCENE III: 221B Baker Street, *morning, two days later*

Characters, in order of appearance:

DR. WATSON

MRS. HUDSON

SHERLOCK HOLMES

INSPECTOR STANLEY HOPKINS: 'An exceedingly alert man, thirty years of age, dressed in a quiet tweed suit, but retaining the erect bearing of one who was accustomed to official uniform.'

JOHN HOPLEY NELIGAN: 'Frail and thin, with black moustache which intensified the deadly pallor of his face. He could not have been much above twenty years of age . . . He was dressed like a gentleman, in Norfolk jacket and knickerbockers, with a cloth cap upon his head.'

JAMES LANCASTER: A seaman. 'A little ribston-pippin of a man, with ruddy cheeks and fluffy white side-whiskers.' Could be North Country.

HUGH PATTINS: A seaman. 'A long, dried-up creature, with lank hair and sallow cheeks.' Irish.

PATRICK CAIRNS: A seaman. Very powerful-looking. 'A fierce, bull-dog face was framed in a tangle of hair and beard, and two bold dark eyes gleamed behind the cover of thick, tufted, overhung eyebrows.'

BLACK PETER

SCENE ONE

[*The parlour of* 221B *Baker Street. This set will remaining standing throughout the play, so here is a chance to present* 221B *in all its immortal clutter.* HOLMES'S *Inverness cape hangs on the wall beside* WATSON'S *topper, frock coat and stethoscope.* WATSON *is seated at the table eating breakfast, the newspaper propped up in front of him.* MRS. HUDSON *enters, carrying a coffee-pot on a tray*]

MRS. HUDSON: Here's some fresh coffee, sir.
WATSON: Ah, thank you, Mrs. Hudson.

[*She sets down the coffee and puts the used pot on her tray*]

MRS. HUDSON: I hope Mr. Holmes isn't off on one of his goose-chases, sir. His breakfast will be quite spoiled.
WATSON: I don't expect he'll be long.

[*He gestures towards the cape*]

Gone out wearing his hat, but not his Inverness. Obviously just a short stroll. [*Pleased with himself*] Deduction, eh?
MRS. HUDSON: Very clever, sir.

[*She goes.* WATSON *returns to his reading, but cannot help glancing again towards the cape, nodding affirmatively and smiling smugly.* HOLMES *enters, wearing his deerstalker which he pulls off and hangs above the cape. He carries a deadly-looking harpoon and moves very energetically*]

HOLMES: Ah, Watson! A very good day to you, my dear fellow!

WATSON [*not looking up from his newspaper*]: Morning, Holmes.

HOLMES: There can be no question, my dear Watson, of the value of exercise before breakfast.

WATSON: Exercise, Holmes? *You?* I don't believe it.

HOLMES: And I return with an excellent appetite. But I'm prepared to bet that you won't guess what form my exercise has taken.

[WATSON *looks up and sees the harpoon for the first time*]

WATSON: Pig-sticking, by the look of it.

HOLMES: Brilliant, Watson. Positively brilliant!

WATSON: Eh? [*Pleased with himself again*] Really, Holmes? No, dash it, you can't go pig-sticking in the middle of the West End.

HOLMES: Nevertheless, that is what I have been doing.

[MRS. HUDSON *enters with her tray, bearing a plate and a covered metal dish*]

And extremely energetic work it proved. Ah, capital, Mrs. Hudson!

[*She places the dish on the table, and the plate in front of* HOLMES, *then exits.* HOLMES *puts the harpoon aside, sits at the table and begins to fill his plate enthusiastically from the dish*]

WATSON: Now, Holmes, no mysteries at this time of the morning, please. What on earth have you been doing with that spear-thing?

HOLMES: Harpoon, Watson. A whaler's harpoon.

[WATSON *gathers some bacon on to his fork*]

I tell you, if you had looked into the back of Allardyce, the butcher's, a few minutes ago, you would have seen a gentleman in his shirtsleeves using it to stab for all he was worth at a dead pig hanging there.

[WATSON, *who had been about to put the bacon into his mouth, pauses, looks with distaste at it, and puts down his fork*]

WATSON [*disgusted*]: No need to ask if that 'gentleman' was you, I suppose?

HOLMES [*eating cheerfully*]: It was. And I have satisfied myself that by no exertion of my strength can I transfix a pig with a single blow of a harpoon. Perhaps you would care to try after breakfast?

WATSON: Certainly not. And if you don't mind, Holmes, I am trying to eat my bacon.

[HOLMES *looks at him, surprised.* MRS. HUDSON *enters*]

MRS. HUDSON: Inspector Stanley Hopkins to see you, sir.

[HOPKINS *enters and* MRS. HUDSON *exits*]

HOLMES: Ah, Hopkins! Come and take some coffee with us.

[HOPKINS *shakes hands with them in turn*]

HOPKINS: Thank you, Mr. Holmes. Morning, Dr. Watson.

WATSON: Morning to you, Inspector.

[HOPKINS *sits at the table.* WATSON *pours for him*]

HOLMES: I expected to see you, but not so early.

HOPKINS: I spent the night in town. I came up yesterday to report back at the Yard.

HOLMES: And what had you to report, Hopkins?

HOPKINS [*gloomily*]: Failure, Mr. Holmes. Absolute failure.

HOLMES: Dear me! I must look at the matter.

WATSON: Holmes, may I ask . . .

HOPKINS: Wish to heavens you would, Mr. Holmes. My first big chance, and I'm at my wits' end.

HOLMES: Well, as it happens, I have read all the available evidence, including the report of the inquest, of course. By the way, what do you make of the tobacco pouch?

[HOPKINS *takes out a leather tobacco pouch and hands it to* HOLMES, *who examines it*]

WATSON: Er, Holmes . . .

HOPKINS: His own, without a doubt. You can see his initials on it.

HOLMES: But he had no pipe, I understand.

HOPKINS: Well, that's true. He didn't smoke. But he might have kept some tobacco for his friends.

WATSON [*louder*]: Holmes, if you don't mind . . .

HOLMES: I only mention it because if I had been handling the case I should have been inclined to make that the starting-point of my investigation. [*Blandly*] Wouldn't you agree, Watson?

WATSON [*beside himself*]: Oh, undoubtedly, Holmes! And now, if you wouldn't mind telling me what on earth you're talking about . . .

HOLMES: Dear me, Hopkins, I was forgetting that my friend Dr. Watson knows nothing of this matter.

WATSON: *Nothing*, Holmes.

HOLMES: I myself should be none the worse for hearing the sequence of events once more. Just give us some short résumé of what you told me over the telephone, will you?

HOPKINS [*amused*]: Very well, sir. You see, Doctor, we've this dead man – Captain Peter Carey, fifty years of age, sealer and whaler. Commanded the ship Sea Unicorn. Did very well. Retired eleven years ago.

WATSON: What? He can't have been forty then.

HOPKINS: Thirty-nine. Travelled about for a few years,

then bought a place near Forest Row, in Sussex, six years ago. Lived there with his wife and daughter aged about twenty. Two female servants. Always changing, and you can't blame them.

WATSON: How so?

HOPKINS: Intermittent drunkard. Perfect fiend when he had the fit on him. Been known to drive his wife and daughter out of doors in the middle of the night and flog them through the park.

WATSON: Great heavens!

HOLMES: It appears, Watson, that he was known as Black Peter in his seafaring days. A graphic description, it seems.

HOPKINS: That's right, Doctor. Huge fellow with a great black beard. Anyway, he built himself a little wooden hut near his house – called it his cabin. All done up with maps and charts, picture of the Sea Unicorn, line of log-books on a shelf, and so on. He slept there every night. Well, last Tuesday he seems to have been in one of his most dangerous moods. Roamed all over the house, drunk and savage, and the womenfolk kept right out of his way. Then he went off to his cabin for the night. Next morning, one of the maids saw the cabin door open, but they were all so afraid of him they didn't venture near till midday.

WATSON: And what did they find?

HOPKINS: Saw it for myself a few hours later, and I can tell you it gave even me a shake. The walls of that hut were like a slaughter-house. Blood everywhere. And there, up against one wall, was Black Peter himself. Pinned upright by a harpoon, right through his chest, like a beetle on a card.

[WATSON *looks round staring at the harpoon, then pushes the covered dish towards* HOLMES]

WATSON [*pointedly*]: Do have some more bacon, Holmes.

HOLMES [*imperturbably*]: Watson, I believe I will.

[*He does*]

WATSON: Ugh!

HOLMES: Tell my friend what you did next, Hopkins.

HOPKINS: Examined the floor and the ground outside. No footmarks.

HOLMES [*eating again*]: Meaning that you saw none.

HOPKINS: There *were* none, sir.

HOLMES: My good Hopkins, I have investigated many crimes, but I have never yet seen one which was committed by a flying creature. As long as the criminal remains upon two legs there must be some indentation, some abrasion, some trifling displacement for the scientific searcher to detect. However, I understand there were *some* things which you did not manage to overlook.

HOPKINS [*draws in his breath*]: The harpoon had been snatched down from a rack on the wall. There were two more there, with 'Sea Unicorn' engraved on them. Carey was fully dressed and there were two empty glasses and a bottle of rum on the table, so I deduced that the crime was done in a moment of fury by some drinking partner. Grabbed the first weapon that came to hand.

WATSON: Sounds plausible enough to me, Inspector.

HOLMES: Yes, I think both inferences are permissible. Tell me, Hopkins, was there any other spirit but rum in the room?

HOPKINS: A tantalus full of brandy and whisky on the sea chest. But I don't see . . .

HOLMES: Then let us hear some more about the things you believe *do* bear on the case.

HOPKINS: The tobacco pouch.

[HOLMES *hands it to* WATSON, *who examines it keenly*]

WATSON: Mm! Some straight-haired skin – sealskin, I suppose. Leather thong to fasten it. Initials P.C. on the flap ... and [*sniffing it*] about half an ounce of strong tobacco in it. Ship's, I should say.

HOLMES: Excellent, Watson! What more, Hopkins?

[HOPKINS *hands over a note-book to* HOLMES]

HOPKINS: This note-book. Found it on the hut floor. Owner's initials J.H.N., and the date 1883 inside the front cover. Several pages of numbers. Mention of Argentina, Costa Rica and San Paulo, and some other fellows' initials – C.P.R.

HOLMES: And what do you make of those?

HOPKINS: Stock Exchange securities. J.H.N. the initials of a broker. C.P.R. those of his client.

HOLMES: By name, Canadian Pacific Railway, no doubt?

HOPKINS: Eh? C.P.R. [*Laughs*] Well, that makes a mug of me, all right. Then, J.H.N. are the only initials we have to worry about. I've been through the old Stock Exchange lists. No one with those initials in the House or among the outside brokers in 1883.

WATSON: Surely, the securities can be traced by their numbers?

HOPKINS: That's true, Doctor. Only, they're South American concerns, and the registers are held over there. I've started enquiries, but it'll take weeks.

HOLMES: Hopkins ...

HOPKINS: Yes, Mr. Holmes? What've you found?

HOLMES: This discoloration on the cover of this note-book. Surely ...

HOPKINS: Blood, sir. I told you, I picked it up off the floor, and there was blood all over the place.

HOLMES: Was this bloodstained side the one uppermost, or next to the boards?

HOPKINS: Next to the boards.

[HOLMES *pushes back his chair and begins to fill his pipe*]

HOLMES: Which proves, of course, that the book was dropped after the crime was committed.

HOPKINS: Exactly, Mr. Holmes. Near the door. Reckon the murderer dropped it as he ran.

HOLMES: And I believe there was also a knife found.

HOPKINS: Also on the floor. Still in its sheath. Mrs. Carey identified it as the Captain's.

WATSON: Inspector, I don't quite see the mystery in all this. I mean, couldn't it be a simple case of intended robbery, in which the thief was surprised by Captain Carey, murdered him, and made off?

HOPKINS: It could, sir – though nothing seems to have been taken, and he could have had his pick with the Captain there dead. Even so, it still leaves us with a murderer to track down.

HOLMES: Which is why you come to me, I suppose?

HOPKINS: I'd be more than obliged for your opinion, Mr. Holmes.

HOLMES [*sighs*]: Ah, well, I suppose I shall have to come out and have a look.

HOPKINS: It'll be a real weight off my mind, sir.

HOLMES: It would have been an easier task a week ago.

HOPKINS [*chidden*]: Yes, sir.

HOLMES: Still, a visit may not be entirely fruitless even now. Watson, if you can spare the time . . .

WATSON: Most certainly, Holmes.

[*They begin to rise from the table*]

HOLMES: Then, if you will call a four-wheeler, Hopkins, we shall be ready to start for Forest Row in a quarter of an hour.

[*Black-out or curtain*]

SCENE TWO

[*A painted drop represents the interior of Captain Carey's 'cabin'. Charts and a picture of the 'Sea Unicorn' on the wall, and a rack for three harpoons, one of which is missing. A shelf littered with books and papers. The only necessary property is a small table, but a couple of small chairs would add to the illusion of reality.* HOLMES *and* WATSON *enter and begin looking round*]

HOLMES: Tell me, Hopkins . . .

[*He turns round to find that* HOPKINS *is not with them.* HOPKINS *enters, looking back at the door*]

HOPKINS: That's a funny thing, Mr. Holmes.

HOLMES: What is it?

HOPKINS: I've just been examining the lock on this door. I'd swear someone's been at it since I was here yesterday.

[HOLMES *goes off to examine the door*]

WATSON: Are there marks?

HOPKINS: Yes, and quite fresh. But whoever it was must have been a pretty poor burglar. He didn't get it open.

WATSON: Some curious villager, perhaps. Eh, Holmes?

HOLMES [*returning*]: I think that fortune is very kind to us. Someone came here expecting to find the door open. He tried to get in with the blade of a very small penknife, but did not succeed. So, what would you expect him to do?

WATSON: Come back the following night – with a more useful implement.

HOLMES: Exactly.

HOPKINS: That's tonight, then.

HOLMES: And it will be our fault if we are not here to receive him. Meanwhile . . .

[He begins to look about again]

HOPKINS: I don't think you'll find anything, Mr. Holmes. I've been over this place with a microscope, almost.

[HOLMES *is examining the shelf of books*]

HOLMES: Have you removed anything from this shelf?

HOPKINS: Nothing, sir.

HOLMES: Something has been taken. There is less dust in this corner of the shelf than elsewhere. It may have been a book lying on its side. It may have been a box. So, Hopkins, let us see what else your microscope failed to reveal, and then we will settle down in patient quiet and see if we cannot come to closer quarters with the gentleman who wished to visit this place last night.

[They all begin examining the room closely. The lighting dims to black-out. We hear the hooting of an owl. The three freeze into waiting attitudes, still in total darkness]

WATSON [*a loud whisper*]: Must be nearly two o'clock, Holmes. [*He yawns*] I tell you, it was probably just some curiosity-monger. He won't come again.

HOLMES [*low*]: Just the same, we must wait and see. Give thanks for a warm night, my dear fellow.

HOPKINS: I reckon we should have left the door ajar for him, Mr. Holmes.

HOLMES: It would only arouse his suspicions. The lock is a perfectly simple one. It needs only a strong blade, and then . . .

[He breaks off as we hear a metallic scraping from the direction of the door]

Ssh! I fancy this is he.

[*More scraping, followed by a snapping sound. We hear the door creak open and see a shaft of lamp-light. It grows as* NELIGAN *enters, holding a lamp aloft. He advances a few paces, but suddenly freezes as his lamp lights up the whole scene and reveals the waiting men*]

HOPKINS [*advancing*]: All right, stay still, or it'll be the worse for you.

NELIGAN [*petrified*]: Wh . . . wh . . . who . . .?

HOPKINS: I'm the police, that's who I am, and this is Mr. Sherlock Holmes. So I'll advise you to say smartly, and with no nonsense, who you may be, and what you think you're doing.

[NELIGAN *slowly puts the lamp down on the table*]

NELIGAN: I . . . You think I'm connected with the death of Captain Peter Carey, I suppose.

HOPKINS: We'll see about that. Let's have your name first, young fellow.

[*He takes out his notebook and writes*]

NELIGAN: It's . . . Neligan. John Hopley Neligan. But I swear I'd nothing to do with the murder.

HOPKINS: John Hopley Neligan? Well, what are you doing here, then?

NELIGAN: Can I speak confidentially?

HOPKINS: No, you can't. You can tell us everything, and quick about it, or it may go badly with you in front of a magistrate.

NELIGAN: Very . . . very well, then. I only want to prevent an old scandal gaining a new lease of life. Did you ever hear of Dawson and Neligan?

HOLMES: The West Country bankers?

NELIGAN: That's right, sir.

HOLMES: They failed for half a million, Hopkins. Ruined half the county families of Cornwall, and Neligan disappeared.

WATSON: I remember, Holmes. Neligan made off with all the securities, didn't he?

NELIGAN: No! Neligan was my father. It isn't true that he stole. He believed that if he were given time to realise the securities, every creditor would be paid in full. He started in his little yacht for Norway, leaving my mother a list of what he'd taken and swearing he'd come back with his honour cleared.

HOPKINS [*disbelieving*]: And did he?

NELIGAN: No.

HOPKINS: Huh!

NELIGAN: Both the yacht and he vanished utterly. We believed, my mother and I, that he, and it, and the securities he'd taken, were at the bottom of the sea. Yet, some time ago, a faithful friend who's a business man discovered that some of the securities had reappeared on the London market. I spent months trying to trace them, and at last I found that the original seller had been Captain Peter Carey.

HOPKINS: You say this is the truth!

NELIGAN: All of it. I made enquiries about Carey and found he'd been in command of a whaler which was due to return from Arctic waters just at the time my father was crossing to Norway. There were many storms that autumn. My father's yacht may well have been blown to the north and met by Carey's ship.

WATSON: Then you suggest that an act of piracy, or something of the sort, took place?

NELIGAN: How can I know what it was? All I know is that my father and his yacht vanished for good, and that in time this Carey sold securities my father had had with him.

HOLMES: Mr. Neligan, what brought you to this place in this clandestine manner?

NELIGAN: I . . . I read of Carey's death. The report stated that the contents of this cabin included the old log-books of his ship, and I hurried here at once, hoping to get my hands on them and find entries for the month in which my father met his fate. I . . . I tried to go about it secretly, so as not to bring an old scandal back to light.

HOLMES: Can you find what you are seeking now?

NELIGAN [*eagerly*]: I'll try.

[*He looks round, sees the shelf of books, and goes to it to search, accompanied by* WATSON *with the lamp*]

[*Suddenly*] This is it!

[*He turns round, holding a small book he would have had concealed about him*]

'1883. January to December.'

[*He riffles quickly through the pages, then stops in the middle, staring*]

HOPKINS: Well, then?

NELIGAN: All the pages for August 1883 are missing. Ripped out. See for yourself.

[*He hands the book to* HOPKINS *who examines it, with* HOLMES *looking over his shoulder*]

HOPKINS: Hm! So, is that all you came for?

NELIGAN: I swear it is.

HOPKINS: And you've never been inside this hut before now?

NELIGAN: That's the truth.

[HOPKINS *whips the note-book out of his pocket*]

HOPKINS [*triumphantly*]: Then how d'you account for this note-book bearing your initials, J.H.N., found lying in the dead man's blood when his body was discovered?

NELIGAN: It . . . it can't have been. I . . . I thought I'd lost it at my hotel.

HOPKINS: Well, here it is, you see, and there's the blood-stain to prove where it was found. So I reckon you'd best save the rest of your talking for the courtroom, and just take a little walk meanwhile with me down to the police station. Mr. Holmes . . .

HOLMES: Yes, Inspector?

HOPKINS: I'm very much obliged to you and your friend in coming down to help me.

HOLMES: Not at all, not at all.

HOPKINS: As it turns out, your presence wasn't necessary. I'd have brought the case to a successful issue without you. All the same, I'm very grateful.

HOLMES: *Thank* you, Inspector. You're too considerate.

HOPKINS: Don't mention it, sir. And I hope we meet again before very long. Now, Neligan, come along, and remember, I'll stand for no trouble on the way.

[*He takes* NELIGAN *by the arm*]

NELIGAN: You shan't have any, I promise.

[HOPKINS *marches off the dejected* NELIGAN]

WATSON [*chuckles*]: Well, Holmes! That's one for you!

HOLMES: Watson, I am disappointed in Stanley Hopkins. I had hoped for better things from him. The first rule of criminal investigation is that one should always look for a possible alternative.

WATSON [*still amused*]: What alternative can there be here?

HOLMES: The line of investigation which I myself have been pursuing. It may give nothing. I cannot tell. But at least I shall follow it to the end.

WATSON: And where does it lead us now, Holmes?

HOLMES: To 221B Baker Street, where I fancy we shall find certain letters awaiting me. Come along my dear fellow.

[WATSON *picks up the lamp. They exit, the stage blacking-out as they go*]

SCENE THREE

[*The parlour of* 221B *Baker Street.* MRS. HUDSON *is clearing away the breakfast things.* HOLMES, *his old dressing-gown over his clothes, is cleaning out his pipe.* WATSON *finishes reading the newspaper and folds it carefully*]

HOLMES: Oh, by the way, Mrs. Hudson . . .

MRS. HUDSON: Yes, sir?

HOLMES: I am expecting Inspector Hopkins here at any moment.

MRS HUDSON: Very well, sir.

HOLMES: And shortly afterwards a number of rough-looking fellows will arrive, asking for 'Captain Basil'. Kindly tell them to wait outside this door until Dr. Watson summons them.

MRS. HUDSON: Yes, sir.

[*She exits with her laden tray*]

WATSON: Captain Basil, Holmes? Who on earth's he?

HOLMES: You will meet him shortly, Watson.

[HOPKINS *enters breezily*]

Ah, Hopkins!

HOPKINS: Morning, Mr. Holmes, Dr. Watson.

WATSON: Morning, Inspector. My word, you're looking breezier than I feel after our late night.

HOLMES: Stimulated by success, no doubt?

HOPKINS: You may be right, sir, you may be right. No, I can't imagine a more complete case.

HOLMES: Your explanation covers every point, then?

HOPKINS: Young Neligan admits he arrived at a hotel in

Forest Row on the very day of the crime. Said he was there to play golf. And he got a room on the ground floor, so's he could go out at any time without being seen. It's plain to me, he went down to Carey's place that night, met the Captain at the hut, quarrelled with him, killed him with the harpoon. Then, horrified by what he'd done, fled out of the hut, dropping the note-book he'd brought with him in order to question Carey about those securities' numbers. After the flight, didn't dare go near the hut again for some time, but at last forced himself to go there after the information he needed.

WATSON: You say he's confessed to all this, Inspector?

HOPKINS: Oh, no. Denies it completely – but I ask you, what could be more obvious?

HOLMES: I must admit that I can see only one drawback to it, Hopkins.

HOPKINS: Well, some slight detail, maybe . . .

HOLMES: And that is that it is intrinsically impossible.

HOPKINS: Eh?

[HOLMES *picks up the harpoon*]

HOLMES: Tell me, have you ever tried to drive a harpoon through a body?

HOPKINS: Drive a . . .! *Course* I haven't!

HOLMES: Tut, tut, my dear fellow, you must really pay attention to these details. My friend Watson will tell you that I spent a whole early morning in that exercise.

WATSON: That's so.

HOLMES: Oh, the body was that of a dead pig, but I can assure you that, although I am stronger than most men, I could not achieve it. It requires an arm that is not only strong, but practised. Now, do you imagine that this anaemic youth was capable of impaling another man to a wall with a weapon such as this?

HOPKINS [*doubtfully*]: Well . . .

HOLMES: Is he the man who hob-nobbed in rum and water with Black Peter in the dead of the night? No, no, Hopkins. We must seek another and a more formidable person.

HOPKINS: Now, look here, Mr. Holmes. You can't deny Neligan was there that night. His note-book being found proves that.

WATSON: It would persuade a jury, Holmes.

HOPKINS: Yes. And besides, I've laid hands on my man. But this other one of yours – where is he?

HOLMES: I rather fancy I hear him on the stairs now.

[*Murmur of gruff voices off-stage*]

HOPKINS: Eh!

HOLMES: Watson, you will find three men outside asking for Captain Basil . . .

HOPKINS: Captain Basil?

HOLMES: . . . Kindly show them in one by one.

WATSON [*moving off*]: Right, Holmes.

[*He goes to the door.* HOLMES *seats himself at the table*]

LANCASTER [*off-stage*]: Cap'n Basil?

WATSON [*off*]: In here, my man. You others wait there.

[LANCASTER *enters, followed by* WATSON, *who indicates* HOLMES *at the table.* LANCASTER *salutes* HOLMES *roughly*]

LANCASTER: Lancaster, sir. James Lancaster.

HOLMES: Hm. I'm sorry, Lancaster. The berth has been filled.

LANCASTER: But . . .

HOLMES: Here's a half-sovereign for your trouble.

[*He produces a coin and hands it over*]

LANCASTER: Much obliged, sir.

HOLMES: Just step into the inside room and wait a few minutes.

LANCASTER [*surprised*]: Right . . . Right ye are, sir.

[WATSON *gestures towards the opposite exit.* LANCASTER *goes*]

HOLMES: Next, Watson.

[WATSON *fetches* PATTINS]

PATTINS: Cap'n Basil, is it?

HOLMES: The same. And you?

PATTINS: Pattins, Cap'n. Hugh Pattins at yer honour's service.

HOLMES: I fear not, Pattins. Here's a half-sovereign instead.

[*He hands it over*]

PATTINS: Here, what the . . .!

HOLMES: Watson, get Lancaster and show the two of them out. They are not to speak to the third man on any account, do you follow?

WATSON: Of course, Holmes.

HOLMES: Then show him in.

WATSON: Very well. [*Calling at the other exit*] Lancaster – come on, now.

LANCASTER [*appearing*]: Aye aye, sir.

WATSON [*to* PATTINS): You, too.

PATTINS [*moving off*]: Ah, what the blazes . . .

[LANCASTER *and* PATTINS *exit, by the door side, followed by* WATSON]

HOPKINS: I wish you'd tell me what all this is, Mr. Holmes.

HOLMES: I will show you instead. [*Low*] Ah!

[CAIRNS *appears, followed by* WATSON. CAIRNS *stands for a moment, taking in the scene, then advances to the table. He does not salute*]

CAIRNS: Name of Cairns. Patrick Cairns.
HOLMES: Cairns? Harpooner?
CAIRNS: Aye. Twenty-six voyages.
HOLMES: And ready to start with an exploring ship?
CAIRNS: Ready enough.
HOLMES: Wages?
CAIRNS: Eight quid a month.
HOLMES: Very well. Your papers, please. [CAIRNS *produces them and tosses them down in front of* HOLMES] Thank you. Hm! Yes, you're just the man I want, Cairns. Here's the agreement. If you'll just read it . . .

[*He hands over a paper.* CAIRNS *leans over to read it, placing both hands on the table to do so.* HOLMES *whips out a pair of handcuffs and claps them on the wrists*]

CAIRNS: What the hell . . .!

[*There is a violent struggle, in which* CAIRNS *manages to seize the harpoon in both hands and menace them. It takes the combined efforts of* HOLMES, WATSON *and* HOPKINS *to subdue him and force him into a chair*]

HOPKINS [*gasping*]: Whew! Strength of a bull!
HOLMES: I thought he was too much for us, even with the handcuffs on.

[CAIRNS *tries to rise, but* HOPKINS *pushes him back*]

CAIRNS: Go to hell!
HOLMES: This is your man, Hopkins. You may arrest him for the murder of Captain Peter Carey.
CAIRNS: Arrest? [*Suddenly deflated*] Cor! Just my luck!
HOPKINS: That's better. Now, sit still and listen. Patrick Cairns, I'm arresting you for the murder of Captain

Peter Carey, and I warn you that anything you say may be given in evidence.

CAIRNS: See here, mister . . . No, I won't give no trouble. But listen. You say I murdered Black Peter. All right – but I say I *killed* him, and that's all the difference in the world.

HOPKINS: Oh, going to sling us some yarn, are you?

CAIRNS: It's no yarn. When he pulled his knife on me I whipped a harpoon through him, sharp. Call that murder, if you like.

HOLMES: We had better hear your story from the beginning before we judge that.

CAIRNS: It was in '83. Black Peter Carey was master of the Sea Unicorn. I was spare harpooner. We'd just come out of the ice-pack, homeward bound, when we picks up a little craft near to foundering. Only one man on her, so we takes him aboard with his tin box.

HOLMES: What was his name?

CAIRNS: I never did hear. He was shut up with the skipper in his cabin for near two days, talking and talking, the ship's boy said. Then, on the second night, the skipper tells the crew the chap's disappeared – fell overboard, he reckons. We never sees him no more.

WATSON: It could have been true, Holmes.

CAIRNS: It could – but it wasn't. Jest one man sees Black Peter tip up that poor chap by his heels over the rail in the dark.

HOLMES: And that man was yourself.

CAIRNS: Right.

HOPKINS: But this was in '83 – twelve years ago. Why didn't you go to the police when you came ashore?

CAIRNS: Because I wanted Black Peter to pay me to keep my mouth shut, that's why. I reckoned there was something in that tin box as'd make it well worth his while – and mine. But he left the sea after that voyage, and it was long years before I could track him down. When I called on him in Sussex a couple of weeks ago he was reasonable and said he'd give me enough to make me free of the sea for life if I'd come back two nights later. So I did. He was three parts drunk this time. We had a rum or two together, but I didn't like the look in his eye. I spotted that harpoon hanging on the wall, and it's as well I did, for he was on to me like a flash.

HOLMES: What did you do after you had killed him?

CAIRNS: I looked around for that tin box. It was on a shelf. I took it down and left the hut, but just as I got outside I heard someone coming. I hid and watched, and saw a man go slinking into the hut. Next minute he gave a great yell and come out, and off as fast as his legs would go.

WATSON: Young Neligan.

CAIRNS: Who?

HOPKINS: Never you mind. What then?

CAIRNS: I walked ten miles to Tunbridge Wells and got a train to London. [*Laughs bitterly*] But when I opened the box there was nothing in it but papers I wouldn't have dared to sell. I'd lost my hold on Black Peter and I was stranded without a shilling. I saw an advertisement by Cap'n Basil for harpooners at high wages . . . and here I am.

HOLMES: A very clear statement.

HOPKINS: Mr. Holmes, I owe you an apology. You were right all along – though I'm blessed if I know how you did it.

HOLMES: All I heard pointed in the one direction. The amazing strength and skill needed to pin a man to a wall with a harpoon; the sealskin tobacco pouch with the coarse tobacco and the initials 'P.C.' . . .

CAIRNS: Here, that must be mine! Where is it?

HOLMES: The Inspector has it. It was found in the hut.

CAIRNS: And I've been wondering where I'd lost it!

HOLMES: The coarse tobacco pointed to a seaman, the sealskin to a whaler. The initials were those of Peter Carey, too, but he seldom smoked and no pipe was found in his cabin. I adjudged that to be a coincidence. Finally, Hopkins, you remember that I asked whether whisky and brandy were in the cabin?

HOPKINS: Yes.

HOLMES: You said they were. How many landsmen are there who would drink rum when they could get these other spirits? Yes, I was certain Carey's visitor had been a seaman. I ascertained the names of the crew of Sea Unicorn in 1883. When I found one Patrick Cairns amongst the harpooners, I advertised that I was signing on hands for an Arctic expedition and offered tempting terms for harpooners who would serve under Captain Basil. Behold the results!

HOPKINS: Wonderful, Mr. Holmes, wonderful!

WATSON: Remarkable, Holmes!

HOLMES: You must obtain the release of young Mr. Neligan as soon as you can, Inspector, even though he lied when he said he had not been in the hut before. I fancy Cairns was telling the truth – that Neligan went in, saw that dreadful sight, and fled.

WATSON: Dropping his note-book.

HOLMES: Precisely. And I think you should waste no time in conveying your prisoner to a place of safety. This room is not well adapted for a cell, and Mr. Patrick Cairns occupies too large a portion of it.

HOPKINS: Yes. Come on, you.

[He jerks CAIRNS *to his feet and marches him off]*

HOLMES: As for ourselves, my dear Watson, I fancy we shall enjoy our morning coffee all the better for having brought our case to a triumphant conclusion.

WATSON: Coffee, *Cap'n Basil*? Shall I ring for Mrs. Hudson, *Cap'n Basil*?

HOLMES: If you please, Mr. Mate.

[*They laugh together as* WATSON *goes over to press the bell, and the curtain falls*]

THE DYING DETECTIVE

SCENE I: Sherlock Holmes's bedroom, *afternoon*
SCENE II: The same, *dusk*
SCENE III: The same, *evening*

Characters, in order of appearance:

MRS. HUDSON

DR. WATSON

SHERLOCK HOLMES

CULVERTON SMITH: 'A great yellow face, coarse-grained and greasy, with heavy double chin, and two sullen, menacing grey eyes which glared at me from under tufted and sandy brows . . .'

INSPECTOR MORTON: Middle-aged, tough, dressed in plain clothes.

THE DYING DETECTIVE

SCENE ONE

[SHERLOCK HOLMES's *bedroom at* 221B *Baker Street. The essential features are: a bed with a large wooden head, placed crosswise on the stage, the head a foot or two from one side wall; a small table near the bed-head, on the audience's side, on which stand a carafe of water and a glass, and a tiny metal or ivory box; a window in the back wall, the curtains parted; and, under the window, a table or chest of drawers, on which stand a green wine bottle, some wine-glasses, a biscuit-barrel, and a lamp. Of course, there may be further lamps and any amount of furnishing and clutter: Holmes's bedroom was adorned with pictures of celebrated criminals and littered with everything from tobacco pipes to revolver cartridges*]

[*There is daylight outside the window.* SHERLOCK HOLMES *lies in the bed on his back, tucked up to the chin and evidently asleep. He is very pale.* MRS. HUDSON *enters followed by* DR. WATSON, *who is wearing his coat and hat and carrying his small medical bag.* MRS. HUDSON *pauses for a moment*]

MRS. HUDSON: He's asleep, sir.

[*They approach the bed.* WATSON *comes round to the audience's side and looks down at* HOLMES *for a moment. He shakes his head gravely, then he and* MRS. HUDSON *move away beyond the foot of the bed.* WATSON *takes off his hat and coat as they talk and she takes them from him*]

WATSON: This is dreadful, Mrs. Hudson. He was perfectly hale and hearty when I went away only three days ago.

MRS. HUDSON: I know, sir. Oh, Dr. Watson, sir, I'm that glad you've come back. If anyone can save Mr. Holmes, I'm sure you can.

WATSON: I shall have to know what is the matter with him first. Mrs. Hudson, please tell me, as quickly as you can, how it all came about.

MRS. HUDSON: Yes, sir. Mr. Holmes has been working lately on some case down near the river – Rotherhithe, I think.

WATSON: Yes, yes. I know.

MRS. HUDSON: Well, you know what he is for coming in at all hours. I was just taking my lamp to go to my bed on Wednesday night when I heard a faint knocking at the street door. I . . . I found Mr. Holmes there. He could hardly stand. Just muttered to me to help him up to his bed here, and he's barely spoken since.

WATSON: Dear me!

MRS. HUDSON: Won't take food or drink. Just lies there, sleeping or staring in a wild sort of way.

WATSON: But, goodness gracious, Mrs. Hudson, why did you not send for another doctor in my absence?

MRS. HUDSON: Oh, I told him straightaway I was going to do that, sir. But he got so agitated – almost shouted that he wouldn't allow any doctor on the premises. You know how masterful he is, Dr. Watson.

WATSON: Indeed. But you could have telegraphed for me.

[MRS. HUDSON *appears embarrassed*]

MRS. HUDSON: Well, sir . . .

WATSON: But you didn't. Why, Mrs. Hudson?

MRS. HUDSON: Sir, I don't like to tell you, but . . . well, Mr. Holmes said he wouldn't even have you to see him.

WATSON: What? This is monstrous! I, his oldest friend, and . . .

[HOLMES *groans and stirs slightly*]

Ssh! He's waking. You go along, Mrs. Hudson, and leave this to me. Whether he likes it or not, I shall ensure that everything possible is done.

MRS. HUDSON: Thank you, sir. You'll ring if I can be of help.

[*She exits with* WATSON'S *things.* HOLMES *groans again and flings out an arm restlessly.* WATSON *comes to the audience's side of the bed and sits on it*]

WATSON: Holmes? It's I – Watson.

HOLMES [*sighs*]: Ahh! Well, Watson? We . . . we seem to have fallen on evil days.

WATSON: My dear fellow!

[*He moves to reach for* HOLMES'S *pulse*]

HOLMES [*urgently*]: No, no! Keep back!

WATSON: Eh?

HOLMES: Mustn't come near.

WATSON: Now, look here, Holmes . . .!

HOLMES: If you come near . . . order you out of the house.

WATSON [*defiantly*]: Hah!

HOLMES: For your own sake, Watson. Contracted . . . a coolie disease – from Sumatra. Very little known, except that most deadly. Contagious by touch. So . . . must keep away.

WATSON: Utter rubbish, Holmes! Mrs. Hudson tells me she helped you to your bed. There's nothing the matter with her.

HOLMES: Period of . . . incubation. Only dangerous after two or three days. Deadly by now.

WATSON: Good heavens, do you suppose such a consideration weighs with me? Even if I weren't a doctor, d'you think it would stop me doing my duty to an old friend? Now, let's have a good look at you.

[*He moves forward again*]

HOLMES [*harshly*]: I tell you to keep back!

WATSON: See here, Holmes ...

HOLMES: If you will stay where you are, I will talk to you. If you will not, you can get out.

WATSON: Holmes! [*Recovering*] Holmes, you aren't yourself. You're sick and as helpless as a child. Whether you like it or not, I'm going to examine you and treat you.

HOLMES [*sneering*]: If I'm to be forced to have a doctor, let him at least be someone I've some confidence in.

WATSON: Oh! You ... After all these years, Holmes, you haven't ... confidence in me?

HOLMES: In your friendship, Watson – yes. But facts are facts. As a medical man you're a mere general practitioner, of limited experience and mediocre qualifications.

WATSON: Well ...! Well, really!

HOLMES: It is painful to say such things, but you leave me no choice.

WATSON [*coldly*]: Thank you. I'll tell you this, Holmes. Such a remark, coming from you, merely serves to tell me what state your nerves are in. Still, if you insist that you have no confidence in me, I will not intrude my services. But what I shall do is to summon Sir Jasper Meek or Penrose Fisher, or any of the other best men in London.

HOLMES [*groans*]: My ... dear Watson. You mean well. But do you suppose they – any of them – know of the Tapanuli Fever?

WATSON: The Tap ...?

HOLMES: What do you yourself know of the Black Formosa Corruption?

WATSON: Tapanuli Fever? Black Formosa Corruption? I've never heard of either of 'em.

HOLMES: Nor have your colleagues. There are many problems of disease, many pathological possibilities, peculiar to the East. So I've learned during some of my recent researches. It was in the course of one of them that I contracted this complaint. I assure you, Watson, you can do nothing.

WATSON: Can't I? I happen to know, Holmes, that the greatest living authority on tropical disease, Dr. Ainstree, is in London just now.

HOLMES [*beseeching*]: Watson!

WATSON: All remonstrance is useless. I am going this instant to fetch him.

[*He gets up*]

HOLMES [*a great cry*]: No!

WATSON: Eh? Holmes ... my dear fellow ...

HOLMES: Watson, in the name of our old friendship, do as I ask.

WATSON: But ...

HOLMES: You have only my own good at heart. Of course, I know that. You ... you shall have your way. Only ... give me time to ... to collect my strength. What is the time now?

[WATSON *sits again and consults his watch*]

WATSON: Four o'clock.

HOLMES: Then at six you can go.

WATSON: This is insanity!

HOLMES: Only two hours, Watson. I promise you may go then.

WATSON: Hang it, this is urgent, man!

HOLMES: I will see no one before six. I will not be examined. I shall resist!

WATSON [*sighing*]: Oh, have it your own way, then. But I insist on staying with you in the meantime. You need an eye keeping on you, Holmes.

HOLMES: Very well, Watson. And now I must sleep. I feel exhausted. [*Drowsily*] I wonder how a battery feels when it pours electricity into a non-conductor?

WATSON: Eh?

HOLMES [*yawning*]: At six, Watson, we resume our conversation.

[*He lies back and closes his eyes.* WATSON *makes as though to move, but thinks better of it. He sits still, watching* HOLMES. *A slow black-out*]

SCENE TWO

[*The stage lights up again, though more dimly than before, to disclose the same scene. Twilight is apparent through the window.* HOLMES *lies motionless.* WATSON *sits as before, though with his head sagging, half-asleep. His chin drops suddenly and he wakes with a jerk. He glances round, sees the twilight outside, and consults his watch. He yawns, flexes his arms, then proceeds to glance idly about him. His attention is caught by the little box on the bedside table. Stealthily, he reaches over and picks it up*]

HOLMES [*very loudly and urgently*]: No! No, Watson, no!

WATSON [*startled*]: Eh? What?

[HOLMES *starts up on to his elbow*]

HOLMES: Put it down! Down this instant! Do as I say, Watson!

WATSON: Oh! All right, then. [*Putting the box down*] Look here, Holmes, I really think . . .

HOLMES: I hate to have my things touched. You know perfectly well I do.

WATSON: Holmes . . .!

HOLMES: You fidget me beyond endurance. You, a doctor – you're enough to drive a patient into an asylum!

WATSON: Really!

HOLMES: Now, for heaven's sake, sit still, and let me have my rest.

WATSON: Holmes, it is almost six o'clock, and I refuse to delay another instant.

[*He gets up determinedly*]

HOLMES: Really? Watson, have you any change in your pocket?

WATSON: Yes.

HOLMES: Any silver?

WATSON [*fishing out his change*]: A good deal.

HOLMES: How many half-crowns?

WATSON: Er, five.

HOLMES [*sighing*]: Ah, too few, too few. However, such as they are, you can put them in your watch-pocket – and all the rest of your money in your left trouser-pocket. It will balance you so much better like that.

WATSON: Balance ... ? Holmes, you're raving! This has gone too far ...!

HOLMES: You will now light that lamp by the window, Watson, but you will be very careful that not for one instant shall it be more than at half flame.

WATSON: Oh, very well.

[WATSON *goes to the lamp and strikes a match*]

HOLMES: I implore you to be careful.

WATSON [*as though humouring him*]: *Yes*, Holmes.

[*He lights the lamp, carefully keeping the flame low. He moves to draw the curtains*]

HOLMES: No, you need not draw curtains.

[WATSON *leaves them and comes back round the bed*]

So! Good. You may now go and fetch a specialist.

WATSON: Well, thank heaven for that.

HOLMES: His name is Mr. Culverton Smith, of 13 Lower Burke Street.

WATSON [*staring*]: Eh?

HOLMES: Well, go on, man. You could hardly wait to fetch someone before.

WATSON: Yes, but ... Culverton Smith? I've never heard the name!

HOLMES: Possibly not. It may surprise you to know that the one man who knows everything about this disease is not a medical man. He's a planter.

WATSON: A planter!

HOLMES: His plantation is far from medical aid. An outbreak of this disease there caused him to study it intensely. He's a very methodical man, and I asked you not to go before six because I knew you wouldn't find him in his study till then.

WATSON: Holmes, I ... I never heard such a ...!

HOLMES: You will tell him exactly how you have left me. A dying man.

WATSON: No, Holmes!

HOLMES: At any rate, delirious. Yes, not dying, delirious. [*Chuckles*] No, I really can't think why the whole ocean bed isn't one solid mass of oysters.

WATSON: Oysters?

HOLMES: They're so prolific, you know.

WATSON: Great Heavens! Now, Holmes, you just lie quiet, and ...

HOLMES: Strange how the mind controls the brain. Er, what was I saying, Watson?

WATSON: You were ...

HOLMES: Ah, I remember. Culverton Smith. My life depends on him, Watson. But you will have to plead with him to come. There is no good feeling between us. He has ... a grudge. I rely on you to soften him. Beg, Watson. Pray. But get him here by any means.

WATSON: Very well. I'll bring him in a cab, if I have to carry him down to it.

HOLMES: You will do nothing of the sort. You will persuade him to come – and then return before him. [*Deliberately*] Make any excuse so as not to come with him. Don't forget that, Watson. You won't fail me. You never did fail me.

WATSON: That's all very well, Holmes, but . . .

HOLMES [*interrupting*]: Then, shall the world be overrun by oysters? No doubt there are natural enemies which limit their increase. And yet . . . No, horrible, horrible!

WATSON [*grimly*]: I'm going, Holmes. Say no more, I'm going!

[*He hurries out.* HOLMES *remains propped up for a moment, staring after* WATSON, *then sinks back into a sleeping posture as the stage blacks out*]

SCENE THREE

[*The stage lights up on the same scene.* HOLMES *lies still. It is now quite dark outside. After a moment* WATSON *bustles in, pulling off his coat. He pauses to hand it to* MRS. HUDSON, *who is behind him*]

WATSON: Thank you, Mrs. Hudson. A gentleman will be calling very shortly. Kindly show him up here immediately.

MRS. HUDSON: Yes, sir.

[*She exits.* WATSON *approaches the bed*]

HOLMES [*drowsily*]: Watson?

WATSON: Yes, Holmes. How are you feeling?

HOLMES: Much the same, I fear. Is Culverton Smith coming?

WATSON: Should be here any minute. It took me some minutes to find a cab, and I almost expected him to have got here first.

HOLMES: Well done, my dear Watson.

WATSON: I must say, Holmes, I'm only doing this to humour you. Frankly, I didn't take to your planter friend at all.

HOLMES: Oh? How so?

WATSON: Rudeness itself. He almost showed me the door before I could give him your message. It wasn't until I mentioned the name, Sherlock Holmes . . .

HOLMES: Ah!

WATSON: Quite changed him – but I wouldn't say it was for the better.

HOLMES: Tell me what he said.

WATSON: Said you'd had some business dealings together, and that he respected your character and talents. Described you as an amateur of crime, in the way that he regards himself as an amateur of disease.

HOLMES: Quite typical – and surely, quite fair?

WATSON: Quite fair – if he hadn't put such sarcasm into saying it. No, Holmes, you said he bears you some grudge. Mark my words, as soon as he has left this house I insist upon calling a recognised specialist.

HOLMES: My dear Watson, you are the best of messengers. Thank you again.

WATSON: Not at all. Holmes, Holmes – let me help you without any of this nonsense. The whole of Great Britain will condemn me otherwise. Why, my cabmen both enquired anxiously after you; and so did Inspector Morton . . .

HOLMES: Morton?

WATSON: Of the Yard. He was passing our door just now as I came in. Seemed extremely concerned.

HOLMES: Scotland Yard concerned for me? How very touching! And now, Watson, you may disappear from the scene.

WATSON: Disappear! I shall do no such thing. I wish to be present when this Culverton Smith arrives. I wish to hear every word of this so-called medical expert's opinion.

HOLMES [*turning his head*]: Yes, of course. Then I think you will just find room behind the head of the bed.

WATSON: What? Hide?

HOLMES: I have reason to suppose that his opinion will be much more frank and valuable if he imagines he is alone with me.

[*We hear the murmur of* MRS. HUDSON'S *and* CULVERTON SMITH'S *voices off-stage*]

Listen! I hear him coming. Get behind the bed, Watson, and do not budge, whatever happens. *Whatever* happens, you understand?

WATSON: Oh, all right, Holmes. Anything to please you. But I don't like this. Not at all.

[*He goes behind the bed-head and conceals himself.* MRS. HUDSON *enters, looks round the room and then at* HOLMES. SMITH *enters behind her*]

MRS. HUDSON [*to* SMITH): Oh, Dr. Watson must have let himself out. No doubt he'll be back directly, sir.

SMITH: No matter, my good woman.

[MRS. HUDSON *bristles at this form of address*]

You may leave me alone with your master.

MRS. HUDSON: As you wish – *sir.*

[*She sweeps out.* SMITH *advances slowly to the bed and stands at the foot, staring at the recumbent* HOLMES]

SMITH [*almost to himself*]: So, Holmes. It has come to this, then.

[HOLMES *stirs.* SMITH *chuckles and leans his arms on the bed-foot and his chin on them, continuing to watch* HOLMES]

HOLMES [*weakly*]: Watson? Who ...? Smith? Smith, is that you?

SMITH [*chuckles*].

HOLMES: I ... I hardly dared hope you would come.

SMITH: I should imagine not. And yet, you see, I'm here. Coals of fire, Holmes – coals of fire!

HOLMES: Noble of you ...

SMITH: Yes, isn't it?

HOLMES: I appreciate your special knowledge.

SMITH: Then you're the only man in London who does. Do you know what is the matter with you?

HOLMES: The same as young Victor – your cousin.

SMITH: Ah, then you recognise the symptoms. Well, then, it's a bad look-out for you. Victor was a strong, hearty young fellow – but a dead man on the fourth day. As you said at the time, it *was* rather surprising that he should contract an out-of-the-way Asiatic disease in the heart of London – a disease of which *I* have made such a very special study. [*Chuckles*] And now, you, Holmes. Singular coincidence, eh? Or are you going to start making accusations once again – about cause and effect, and so on.

HOLMES: I . . . I knew you caused Victor Savage's death.

[SMITH *comes round the bed*]

SMITH [*snarling*]: Did you? Well, proving it is a different matter, Holmes. But what sort of a game is this, then – spreading lying reports about me one moment, then crawling to me for help the next?

HOLMES [*gasping*]: Give . . . give me water. For . . . pity's sake, Smith. Water!

[SMITH *hesitates momentarily, then goes to the table and pours a glass from the carafe*]

SMITH: You're precious near your end, my friend, but I don't want you to go till I've had a word with you.

[*He holds out the glass to* HOLMES *who struggles up feebly to take it and drinks*]

HOLMES [*gulping water*]: Ah! Thank . . . thank you. Please . . . do what you can for me. Only cure me, and I promise to forget.

SMITH: Forget what?

HOLMES: About Victor Savage's death. You as good as admitted just now that you had done it. I swear I will forget it.

SMITH [*laughs*]: Forget it, remember it – do as you like. I don't see you in any witness-box, Holmes. Quite another shape of box, I assure you. But you must hear first how it came about.

HOLMES: Working amongst Chinese sailors. Down at the docks.

SMITH: Proud of your brains, aren't you? Think yourself smart? Well, you've met a smarter one this time.

[HOLMES *falls back, groaning loudly*]

Getting painful, is it?

[HOLMES *cries out, writhing in agony*]

SMITH: That's the way. Takes you as cramp, I fancy?

HOLMES: Cramp! Cramp!

SMITH: Well, you can still hear me. Now, can't you just remember any unusual incident – just about the time your symptoms began?

HOLMES: I ... can't think. My mind is gone! Help me, Smith!

SMITH: Did nothing come to you through the post, for instance?

HOLMES: Post? Post?

SMITH: Yes. A little box, perhaps?

HOLMES [*a shuddering groan*].

SMITH [*closer; deadly*]: Listen! You *shall* hear me! Don't you remember a box – a little ivory box? [*He sees it on the table and holds it up*] Yes, here it is on your bedside table. It came on Wednesday. You opened it – do you remember?

HOLMES: Box? Opened? Yes, yes! There was ... sharp spring inside. Pricked my finger. Some sort of joke ...

SMITH: It was no joke, Holmes. You fool! Who asked you to cross my path? If you'd only left me alone I would never have hurt you.

HOLMES: Box! Yes! Pricked finger. Poison!

SMITH [*triumphantly*]: So you do remember. Good, good! I'm glad indeed. Well, the box leaves this room in my pocket, and there's your last shred of evidence gone. [*He pockets it*] But you have the truth now, Holmes. You can die knowing that I killed you. You knew too much about what happened to Victor Savage, so you must share his fate. Yes, Holmes, you are very near your end now. I think I shall sit here and watch you die.

[*He sits on the bed*]

HOLMES [*almost a whisper*]: The ... shadows ... falling. Getting ... so dark. I can't see. Smith! Smith, are you there? The light ... for charity's sake, turn up the light!

[SMITH *laughs, gets up and goes to the light*]

SMITH: Entering the valley of the shadow, eh, Holmes? Yes, I'll turn up the light for you. I can watch your face more plainly, then. [*He turns the flame up full*] There! Now, is there any *further* service I can render you?

HOLMES [*in a clear, strong voice*]: A match and my pipe, if you please.

[*He sits bolt upright.* SMITH *spins round to see him*]

SMITH: Eh? What the devil's the meaning of this?

HOLMES [*cheerfully*]: The best way of successfully acting a part is to *be* it. I give you my word that for three days I have neither tasted food nor drink until you were good enough to pour me out that glass of water. But it's the tobacco I find most irksome.

[*We hear the thud of footsteps running upstairs off-stage*]

Hello, hello! Do I hear the step of a friend?

[INSPECTOR MORTON *hurries in*]

MORTON: Mr. Holmes?

HOLMES: Inspector Morton, this is your man.

SMITH: What is the meaning of . . .?

MORTON: Culverton Smith, I arrest you on the charge of the murder of one Victor Savage, and I must warn you that anything you say . . .

SMITH: You've got nothing on me! It's all a trick! A pack of lies!

[*He makes to escape.* MORTON *restrains him*]

MORTON: Keep still, or you'll get yourself hurt!

SMITH: Get off me!

MORTON: Hold your hands out!

[*They struggle.* MORTON *gets out handcuffs and claps them on* SMITH'S *wrists*]

That'll do.

HOLMES: By the way, Inspector, you might add the attempted murder of one Sherlock Holmes to that charge. Oh, and you'll find a small box in the pocket of your prisoner's coat. Pray, leave it on the table, here. Handle it gingerly, though. It may play its part at his trial.

[MORTON *retrieves the box and places it on the table*]

SMITH: Trial! You'll be the one in the dock, Holmes. Inspector, he asked me to come here. He was ill, and I was sorry for him, so I came. Now he'll pretend I've said anything he cares to invent that will corroborate his insane suspicions. Well, you can lie as you like, Holmes. My word's as good as yours.

HOLMES: Good heavens! I'd completely forgotten him!

MORTON: Forgotten who, sir?

HOLMES: Watson, my dear fellow! Do come out!

[WATSON *emerges with cramped groans*]

I owe you a thousand apologies. To think that I should have overlooked you!

WATSON: It's all right, Holmes. Would have come out before, only you said, whatever happened, I wasn't to budge.

SMITH: What's all this about?

HOLMES: I needn't introduce you to my witness, my friend Dr. Watson. I understand you met somewhat earlier in the evening.

SMITH: You ... you mean you had all this planned?

HOLMES: Of course. To the last detail. I think I may say it worked very well – with your assistance, of course.

SMITH: Mine?

HOLMES: You saved an invalid trouble by giving my signal to Inspector Morton, waiting outside. You turned up the lamp.

[SMITH *and* WATSON *are equally flabbergasted*]

MORTON: I'd better take him along now, sir. [*To* SMITH] Come on.

[*He bundles* SMITH *roughly towards the door*]

We'll see you down at the Yard tomorrow, perhaps, Mr. Holmes?

HOLMES: Very well, Inspector. And many thanks.

WATSON: Goodbye, Inspector.

[MORTON *exits with* SMITH]

[*Chuckles*] Well, Holmes?

HOLMES: Well, Watson, there's a bottle of claret over there – it is uncorked – and some biscuits in the barrel. If you'll be so kind, I'm badly in need of both.

[WATSON *goes to fetch them*]

WATSON: Certainly. You know, Holmes, all this seems a pretty, well, elaborate way to go about catching that fellow. I mean, taking in Mrs. Hudson – *and me* – like that. Scared us half to death.

HOLMES: It was very essential that I should make Mrs. Hudson believe in my condition. She was to convey it to you, and you to him.

WATSON: Well . . .

HOLMES: Pray do not be offended, my good Watson. You must admit that among your *many* talents, dissimulation scarcely finds a place. If you'd shared my secret, you would never have been able to impress Smith with the urgent necessity of coming to me. It was the vital point of the whole scheme. I knew his vindictive nature, and I was certain he would come to gloat over his handiwork.

[WATSON *returns with the bottle, glasses and barrel*]

WATSON: But . . . but your appearance, Holmes. Your face! You really do look ghastly.

HOLMES: Three days of absolute fast does not improve one's beauty, Watson. However, as you know, my habits are irregular, and such a feat means less to me than to most men. For the rest, there is nothing that a sponge won't cure. Vaseline to produce the glistening forehead; belladonna for the watering of the eyes; rouge over the cheekbones and crust of beeswax round one's lips . . .

WATSON [*chuckling*]: And that babbling about oysters!

[*He begins pouring the wine*]

HOLMES: Yes. I've sometimes thought of writing a monograph on the subject of malingering.

WATSON: But why wouldn't you let me near you? There was no risk of infection.

HOLMES: Whatever I may have said to the contrary in the grip of delirium, do you imagine that I have no respect for your medical talents? Could I imagine that you would be deceived by a dying man with no rise of pulse or temperature? At four yards' distance I *could* deceive you.

[WATSON *reaches for the box*]

WATSON: This box, then . . .

HOLMES: No, Watson! I wouldn't touch it. You can just see, if you look at it sideways, where the sharp spring emerges as you open it. I dare say it was by some such device that poor young Savage was done to death. He stood between that monster and an inheritance, you know.

WATSON: Then it's true, Holmes! You . . . you might have been killed, too!

HOLMES: As you know, my correspondence is a varied one. I am somewhat on my guard against any packages which reach me. But I saw that by pretending he had succeeded in his design I might be enabled to surprise a confession from him. That pretence I think I may claim to have carried out with the thoroughness of a true artist.

WATSON [*warmly*]: You certainly did, Holmes. Er, a biscuit?

[*He holds out the barrel*]

HOLMES: On second thoughts, Watsons, no thank you. Let us preserve our appetite. By the time I have shaved and dressed, I fancy it will just be nice time for something nutritious at our little place in the Strand.

[*They raise their glasses to one another and drink. The curtain falls*]